Meeting Jesus

William P. Sampson

HarperSanFrancisco
A Division of HarperCollinsPublishers

Scriptural quotations unless otherwise noted are my own. Scriptural quotations marked NJB are from or based upon The New Jerusalem Bible, copyright © 1985; those marked JB are from or based upon The Jerusalem Bible,
copyright © 1966 by Doubleday, a division of Bantam, Doubleday, Dell
Publishing Group, Inc., and by Darton, Longman, & Todd, Ltd., and used by
permission of the publishers. Those marked NEB are from or based upon
The New English Bible, copyright © 1961, 1970 by the Delegates of the
Oxford University Press and the Syndics of the Cambridge University Press.
Those marked RSV are from or based upon The Revised Standard Version,
copyright © 1952, 1971 by the Division of Christian Education of the
National Council of the Churches of Christ. Those marked NAB are from
or based upon The New American Bible, copyright © 1971, 1976 by The
Confraternity of Christian Doctrine.

Where it was useful, I changed 'Yahweh' to 'Lord', the past tense to the
present, and an occasional phrase for the purpose of inclusivity.

FIRST EDITION

This edition is printed on acid-free paper that meets the American National
Standards Institute Z39.48 Standard.

Library of Congress Cataloging-in-Publication Data

Sampson, William P.
    Meeting Jesus / William P. Sampson. — 1st ed.
        p. cm.
    ISBN 0-06-067033-9 (alk. paper)
     1. Jesus Christ — Biography — Devotional literature. 2. Jesus
Christ — Character. I. Title.
BT306.5.S32 1991
232.9 — dc20

90-55799
CIP

91 92 93 94 95 VICKS 10 9 8 7 6 5 4 3 2 1

Foreword

Jesus remains elusive as ever, but William Sampson nonetheless aims daringly at a genuine "meeting." His term "meeting," however, is freighted with dangerous inventiveness. As an experienced teacher, Sampson has concluded that there can be no "meeting" with Jesus, neither by fixed, settled theological categories nor through critical attempts to recover and specify the historical Jesus. Thus Sampson takes up his quest at the place where the old approaches are in doubt.

What to do? Sampson turns from teaching to directing retreats. In this move he not only changes venues but also changes method and perspective. In the new context of reflective retreat, this book leads one on a journey of imagination, daring to voice what it must have been like to be Jesus. What is offered then are probes into the various seasons of life on the journey and career of Jesus who, only through time, "uncovers his identity at the center of human history."

Sampson's imaginative venture combines a searching awareness of scripture, a firm grasp of the history of Jesus' time, and a shrewd eye on the contemporaneity of his reader. His treatment of Jesus is no doubt open to the charge of subjectivism, as he knows full well. He is, in the face of such a charge, struggling with the more seductive problem of objectivism that makes no contact and permits no "meeting" with Jesus.

Without any labored theoretical statement, this book practices a hermeneutic that moves back and forth between the live memory of Jesus and the situation of the reader. Only so is a "meeting" possible that can impact both parties.

The outcome of such a procedure is a process of struggling with Jesus that will let a meeting happen, a meeting that depends upon and powerfully appeals to the legitimacy of imagination. The book is, of course, open for criticism of such a hermeneutical maneuver, which parts company with much historical study.

Sampson exhibits no defensiveness about his approach. I imagine he would only insist that so-called objective portrayals of Jesus constitute only a duller consensus wrought out of imagination. Sampson's concern is not only knowledge about Jesus but transformation, the kind of transformation that happens only in a "meeting." The book will not please a lot of scholars. It will, I think, mediate Jesus to a lot of readers. I imagine Jesus would have willingly joined such an enterprise — parables and all.

Walter Brueggemann, President
Society of Biblical Literature, 1990
Columbia Theological Seminary

iv

Preface

What must it have been like to meet Jesus? To answer that the Gospels were written. To convey some idea of what it was like to be around him is one important reason the evangelists wrote.

"What was it like to live with Charlie?" "Well, it was a lot like living next door to a firehouse!" Or "It was like living with a hyperactive child."

In describing what it is like to meet someone, we also describe what she is like, what is going on within her. So too the evangelists depict Jesus' own experience at this moment and at that moment as he goes from day to day.

Of course, it is all in retrospect. What had it been like to meet him who later rose from the dead? That retrospective viewpoint influenced their description. I am seeking to eliminate as much of that influence as possible, to catch him as he lived from day to day.

In this book, I am involved in inventing. "Inventing a probable past," in the words of novelist Thomas Fleming. It is a task for the imagination. Fleming is reviewing a book on James Fenimore Cooper by Sewall Cushing Stout, Jr. Stout uses the term *veracious imagination* as an effort to "deepen and broaden art's penetration of reality." It is a world of probables and less probables. My effort is to select and flesh out a probable development within Jesus as he matures.

Can we reconstruct this maturing in any meaningful way? It is very similar to the task that critics take up when they try to capture the origin and development of a work of literature. They discover the choices that are contained in the final version and the alternatives that were rejected and are not in the final version. The play of the artist's freedom is revealed in the movement from the first inspirations to the final form.

What was it like for Jesus to undergo this maturing, to be confronted with choices, to have the burden of freedom and its enjoyment, to live in the darkness that surrounds human choice?

What was it like for him to be faced with the unknown, the unheard of, the unexpected?

I have been much encouraged and helped in this work by Francis Schemel and James Walsh, both Jesuits of Georgetown University, and good friends.

I have also been helped by the many sisters who—in my desire to help them imagine Jesus more and more realistically—motivated me along this path. Especially am I grateful to those sisters who trusted in me over the years—so many of them; let me name but two: Sister Mary Catherine Kenny of Bethany, Highland Mills, New York, and Sister Immaculata of Westview in Pittsburgh. From them I acquired the hope that this work will help others.

Introduction

In the 1960s the Catholic church went through many changes. One of them involved changing the style of the annual retreat, the six- or eight-day obligation of most members of religious orders. The earlier format involved one man giving three or four talks each day to many people. After each talk the retreatants would pray about the matter presented. The weakness of this method had long been felt, and many new avenues were being explored.

One of these was the directed retreat. Here a single retreat director sees a single retreatant each day privately, once or twice. The matter presented is still the basic gospel dynamic, but it is tailored to the retreatant's needs. Problems particular to this retreatant can be dwelt on. I was very impressed by it when I first saw it being done.

I made a thirty-day retreat of this type in 1969. I was an English teacher, and I was especially attracted to this type of retreat by the emphasis it placed on the imagination. Along with many others, I had become convinced that Jesuit education had lost much of its focus. After centuries of working with the imagination as well as the intellect and the memory, it had largely lost its expertise in developing the student's imagination. In teaching English, I had put all my energies into that task: how to encourage students to use more than just their reasoning powers and memory.

How do you test the imagination? That was the challenge, and I found it absorbing. The delight the students experienced as they liberated their imaginations was a great reward. I was discovering for myself that the imagination's grasp on the particular details was the key to all learning.

The directed retreat had a similar focus. The prayer exercises centered on an imagined scene from the Gospels. The retreatant was invited and helped to enter that scene vividly, as a participant, and to let the imagination take its own course. It brought into play much deeper levels of the personality, areas that tend to be hidden from us.

About twenty years ago I switched from teaching to giving directed retreats. I directed my first retreatants in 1970, and my experiences over the years eventually led to this book.

Quite a few retreatants see themselves as having no imagination. Through the contemporary presentation of the Spiritual Exercises of Ignatius Loyola, however, they can be enabled to discover their imagination and to experience its immense power. Through the imagination, reality can be entered at depths not available to our reasoning powers. The gospel message can come alive with unparalleled force, and an experience similar to the one the apostles had can touch us.

This book aims at just such a goal: to help people encounter Jesus just as the apostles did — in the midst of that series of decisions through which Jesus discovered and became himself.

Because Christianity centers not on a series of statements or a list of commandments but on a person who lived out his human life on planet earth, Christians have always been fascinated by the particulars of this man's life. The four Gospels were written in part to satisfy that desire. Each contains a way of looking at Jesus, of imagining what he must have been like.

What did he do first? What was it like in the beginning? What happened next? How did he feel? In this way we shape our image of what his experience was like. All this helps us in getting at that most important question, How would he relate to me were he present today?

If my image of Christ is minimal, if he remains a shadowy, remote figure, hard to decipher or imagine, my experience of him will be far from the experience that his first followers had. I really won't know him. The purpose of the Gospels was to convey to those who heard them what the apostles experienced. That is the goal of this book.

Today scholars are reluctant to present any image of Jesus at all. They feel that the historical data are inadequate for establishing any certitude about him. This has left the field wide open for Hollywood and the novelists. But the Jesus that is presented in movies such as *The Last Temptation of Christ* can strike many believers as implausible and not true to the Gospels.

I have tried to imagine Jesus as realistically as possible and yet do justice to gospel faith. I am presenting Jesus as he develops through the course of his life as he goes from problem to problem and choice to choice, until he enters into an awareness of his divinity.

I portray him not as a failed revolutionary or a confused do-gooder badly misinterpreted by his followers or as a visitor from outer space. I portray him as a person who, step by step, uncovers his identity at the center of human history.

In directing retreats and listening to the retreatant's efforts to imagine what it was like to be present at a Gospel event, I repeatedly encountered a major difficulty. The retreatant often imagined that Jesus was conscious of his divinity and was able to read the minds of all around him through his divine powers. Often the retreatant would imagine herself praying to Jesus in the scene for help with some personal problem that Jesus knew all about without having to be told. Of course, the Gospel event was lost sight of.

How do you relate to someone who was present at your creation and knows everything there is to know about your past, present, and future? We really don't know how to respond, and the people who lived with Jesus did not have that problem. That was not how he came across.

Early on I began inviting people to imagine a thoroughly human Jesus, one who could not read minds and who did not yet know the future in all its details. This Jesus would have lived out his life in the dark and would have been forced to make choices as life moved forward without any clear map, just the way all other human beings operate.

Ordinarily this suggestion led to a much more gripping image of Jesus and to vivid imagining. Jesus remained utterly unique but imaginable.

That conviction forms the basis of the book. What I do, then, is to present a series of moments in Jesus' life, moments when he was confronted with a choice. These are portrayed in some detail. I suggest the problems that faced him and portray him as deciding on a solution in the same darkness that accompanies all human decision making.

I suggest the alternatives that confronted him in an effort to show that his choice was not an inevitable one. The alternatives that presented themselves to him were reasonable ones. In retrospect we can ignore them, but we then leave out of our picture the experience he had.

What was going on inside him that propelled him into preaching rather than becoming a local rabbi? Was there a period when he felt called to be a second John the Baptist, called to finish the work that had been interrupted by the Baptist's death? When he did decide to preach, what message did he choose to highlight? What was it that made him change his focus as time went by?

We are inside Jesus, so, of course, our answers are projections. Even where there is an autobiography to work with, we still can only conjecture when describing the inner life of the person. With Jesus we don't even have an autobiography.

We do have the New Testament. Scholars have examined it with massive effort. Tools have been developed, especially in the last hundred years, to assign levels of possibility and probability to items and sayings and events. Sometimes a consensus develops and persists about a particular item, but often scholars disagree sharply, and at times a consensus that had been formed falls apart as time passes.

I did not feel obliged to follow the majority opinion. I did feel obliged to use some respected scholarship in support of the items that involve a certain expertise. I selected those details that fitted my own sense of plausibility, as long as there was some support among the scholars that this was a possible, even a probable, scenario.

The second criterion I used was my own belief. I do believe that Jesus is God, the Son. I do believe that he never made a sinful choice. I also believe that Jesus became aware of his divine identity before the crucifixion. He was the first to grasp the full nature of his own place as the redeemer of all through his life and death.

Using these two criteria, I have projected what it was like to be Jesus, what his inner experience was.

Galileo was thought to be the first human being ever to turn a telescope up to the night sky. He wrote in his dairy what it was like to have his whole world turned upside down by the moons of Jupiter. It makes fascinating reading.

Jesus was the first Christian. It was inside his consciousness that the spectacular good news was first heard and understood in its fullness. What was it like for a human consciousness to become aware of the secret hidden from the foundation of the world? What was it like for a human consciousness to become aware that it itself was a divine reality? That is what this book tries to imagine, the gradual process by which the good news found a home within this one man's mind and heart and thereby entered human history.

As the early followers of Jesus struggled to understand what they had witnessed in their encounter with him, one of them expressed it this way:

> Something which has existed since the beginning,
> that we have heard,
> and we have seen with our own eyes;
> that we have watched
> and touched with our hands . . . (1 John 1:1)

This was his effort to grasp what had occurred. But what had happened was basically indescribable, so we end up with a passage that is largely incoherent. It is filled with grammatical contradictions.

A commentator casts light on the reason for the difficult style. It is a passage, he says, "more remarkable for energy than for lucidity."* This was what the writer was reaching for—energy. Something unparalleled had occurred. He needed a new language. So he calls that very human companion whom he had touched with his own hands a "something." We say, "She was really something!" "Isn't he something else!"

The disciple had met a newness without parallel. An energy had invaded his life that was hard to describe. But he was not the first to be faced with the problem of how to grasp the event that was this person Jesus. No, it was Jesus himself who was the forerunner, the first to enter through the breach, the first to glimpse the newly exposed heart of reality.

What was it like to be him?

We shall seek to throw some flesh on the bare bones of our knowledge of Jesus' inner life. We shall track him through his childhood first. We shall be suggesting various likely scenarios. Some may strike you as implausible, even impossible, but some may ring

---

*Alfred Loisy, *Les Epîtres dites de Jean*, in *Le Quatrième Evangile* (Paris: Nourry, 1921), 531; cited in Raymond E. Brown, S. S., *Epistles of John*, Anchor Bible Series, no. 30, (Garden City, NY: Doubleday, 1982), 152.

true for you and appear likely and even stimulating, capturing some hint of what it must have been like.

We do not know much about the particulars of his early life. But we know it was filled with particulars, as our own lives are. To gain some awareness of what his actual experience must have been, all we can do is try out some likely scenes. They can help make Jesus come alive in our imagination. Their purpose is to help grasp the full flavor of his experience rather than to contend that this is the way it must have happened.

Jesus lived out his life as we do—from one concrete setting to another, one choice to another.

This is how I envision it must have been.

Chapter One

As a child of Nazareth Jesus does a lot of memorizing. There is just one copy of the Scriptures in the village, that of the rabbi, kept in the synagogue. Only gradually does Jesus hear the Law and the Prophets, as it is read out in class and commented on and reread and memorized. A day comes when he hears for the first time the story of Jonah. Someone reads aloud, perhaps the rabbi himself:

> The word of the LORD was addressed to Jonah, son of Amittai: "Up!" he said, "Go to Nineveh." (Jon. 1:1 NJB)

What is it like for him to hear it? Well, we can begin with, What is it like for any Jewish student of his day? To help understand the concerns of the youth of his day, let us look at a bit of history.

We need not go back to Adam; Alexander the Great will make a good starting point. Over three hundred years before Jesus' day, Alexander had conquered Israel and all the lands nearby. He had brought with him Greek culture—the Greek taste in architecture and sculpture, the Greek language, the Greek eagerness for sports and drama, Greek poetry and plays, and the Greek gods.

It was very attractive and it caught on. If you wanted to build a new city hall, you brought in a Greek architect. If you wanted to be cultured, you learned Greek. Your children needed a Greek tutor.

If you were wealthy enough, your boys were sent to Athens for their education. You might even have a statue of Mars in your home. In Jerusalem a stadium was built. There the young Jewish boys could imitate Greek athletes. A theater was constructed where Greek plays could be performed. It sounds strange—a stadium and a theater in the Jerusalem of Jesus' day—but such Greek influences played a large part in Palestinian Jewish life.

1

There were some devout Israelites who did not like this un-Jewish invasion. They feared that it would lead to a loss of faith in Yahweh. Hadn't this openness to other religions been a cause of Israel's disgrace in the past? To them it appeared that national apostasy was coming on fast.

What could be done about it? Those disturbed by the Greek trend were mostly laity, not the religious leaders. The leaders were the very ones whose wealth sucked them into this new fashion. Those who controlled the temple, and derived their wealth from it, were not aware of the danger threatening Israel. There was no hope that the priests would lead a return to the true worship of Yahweh. A reform would have to take place apart from the temple.

In each village a teacher was provided. He instructed the people each week in the Law and the Prophets. In each village there was a copy of the Scriptures. There was a meeting place, a classroom where this instruction took place. Special classes were given to boys from the age of seven to about twelve. Some continued their studies until they were much older. These lay reformers had invented the synagogue, for that is what the classroom was called. The teacher was called the rabbi. The reform was very successful. It even influenced the priesthood.

Such was the beginning of the Pharisees, the lay reformers. In the Nazareth of Jesus' day, there is a synagogue where everyone is instructed each Sabbath in the Law and the Prophets. Each week new lessons and new instruction are given by the rabbi. For the young Jesus there are classes during the week with other boys. Over the years he hears the whole of the Law and the Prophets. Jesus is educated by the Pharisees. He encounters the temple people, the priests, the Sadducees, only on occasional visits to Jerusalem.

The Pharisees are looked upon with great reverence by the devout. They had saved Israel from a new exile. They had brought the people back to respect the Law and to know the Prophets.

There were some people who felt that even this was not enough. They were convinced that the just must separate themselves from the unjust so that they will not perish with them. About 150 years before the birth of Jesus they built a monastery in a desert area overlooking the Dead Sea, the monastery of Qumran. There they lived intensely focused on the coming of the end of the world.

2

They went to great lengths to keep themselves ready. Purification rituals involving water and bathing played a large part in their lives.

The monastery had been destroyed by an earthquake about thirty years before Jesus was born, but it was rebuilt about the time of his birth. Jesus hears of it, and in his teens, on a visit to Jerusalem, he visits there. It is but a two-hour walk from Jericho.

It is an impressive place. The order and dignity of the life, the calm but intense anticipation of the coming of the great Day of the Lord. It is very attractive. Outsiders visit and even spend days of retreat there. There are children too, children whose parents handed them over to the monks to be raised at the monastery. Day after day of regular order, study, prayer, liturgical rites, ritual meals, daily labor, the crops from a freshwater spring below, the water supply to be cared for—it is very attractive.

This daily schedule centering around a coming event is designed to further the mood of anticipation. A great day is coming, and only a fool will ignore it. To live each day in total readiness, that is true wisdom. A vast overturn is about to take place, and the powers of the world are about to be shaken. It is vital to be a part of the faithful remnant that will be raised up on that dark day.

It is a rather rare phenomenon in human history—when a whole people is gripped by a sense that something suprahistorical is about to happen, that history is coming to an end. It happened again around the year A.D. 1000. It is present, oddly enough, in our own day, as the third millennium approaches. It produces a literature filled with imaginative efforts to describe what this future event will be like. The mood is apocalyptic: an anticipation of a dramatic intervention into human history from outside, an intervention that will radically overturn the ways our lives are lived.

In our own day we see it in science fiction. So filled are we with expecting an intervention from outside that people are seeing it happen. Each month there is another UFO sighting. Our films and novels try to picture what it will be like: 2001, E.T., Close Encounters of the Third Kind. Religious and other groups prepare with total dedication for the end of the world—Armageddon.

In Jesus' day, it is not just at the monastery of Qumran that this mood is present. As Jesus is growing up, he encounters that mood even in his village. It is everywhere. Certain Scripture texts that had been buried for centuries are now on everyone's lips. That the great day—the Day of the Lord—is very near is a general conviction. Certain figures are supposed to appear during the last days. People are looking for them.

If we were to see an odd-looking character wandering in a field, we might wonder what galaxy he has come from and how it came about that he fell to earth. But in Jesus' day they ask whether he is one of the great persons who are scheduled to arrive in the last days—the prophet, Moses, Elijah, or the messiah. Great personages are due to arrive soon, although no one agrees on particulars.

What is it like for Jesus to hear a passage like this:

> That day—it is the Lord GOD who speaks—
> I will make the sun go down at noon,
> and darken the earth in broad daylight.
> I am going to turn your feasts into funerals.
> (Amos 8:9–10 JB)

Perhaps you know a sci-fi addict, his imagination infested with scripts for the future. His ancient counterparts are everywhere in Jesus' day. People are filled with expectation.

In many respects Jesus is a typical student of his day, and his experiences and reactions are like theirs. But in some respects he has a very different experience.

Why is that? The young Jesus has something that is not present in the other students' lives. It is his actual sinlessness. He is tempted as they are, but his choice is for love and faith. The desire to resent or to avenge never gets its way with him. At the deepest and most hidden levels of his being is a spontaneity for God's will that expresses itself in an affection for people, a compassion, a persistent forgiving, a reluctance to judge.

This is a fact of Jesus' life that we touch only in faith. What does this reality feel like for Jesus? What is it like to grow up sinless in a world filled with sinners?

Early on Christians tried to imagine his experience. Here is one effort, and although it tries to describe his total experience, the image it presents can be applied to his early years.

> Jesus says: I stood up in the midst
> of the world, and I revealed myself

4

to them in the flesh, and I found
them all drunk; and I found no one
among them who was thirsty; and my
soul is in pain over the sons of
men, because they are blind in
their hearts and see not they are
poor and do not realize their
poverty.*

Here is an example.

You arrive at the office Christmas party rather late. No one has left yet, and everyone is quite happy by now. You join a laughing group. There's a childish remark at which everyone explodes with laughter. Then a half-word and they laugh again uncontrollably. You wander over to two other people. Mumblings you cannot quite hear. All about love. Half-intelligible assurances of affection. Mostly vulgarity, but they are deeply engaged in this soul sharing and delighting in their new discovery of each other.

It can be very painful for you. So too for Jesus. To be so clear-headed in the presence of such confusion, so honest in the midst of such lying, to be so filled with affection in the midst of such antagonism, animosity, and competitiveness, to be so real in the midst of such phoniness. His heart is moved to identify with this sad people. They are his. He belongs to them.

When someone who belongs to you is an alcoholic, how much it demands; how strong the temptation to turn away, to ignore him. Friends tell you, "Forget him. It's the best thing you can do for both of you."

It is much like that in a parable from the early Fathers. In ambling over the earth, God has come upon the body of Abel. God is shocked, having never imagined such a turn of events — a brother has murdered his brother. Back in heaven, God reveals what has happened to the angelic counselors, and they urge God to abandon this race altogether, to start all over again with a new beginning.

---

* *The Coptic Gospel of Thomas,* logion 28, in Herbert Musurillo, S.J., *The Fathers of the Primitive Church* (New York: New American Library, 1966), 121.

At times that temptation comes to us: it's too much of a mess, Lord; there's nothing worth saving here.

But Jesus, like his Father, chooses to move voluntarily into deeper affection for people. Here his vocation begins, in his refusal to turn away, in his deliberately linking his life with theirs. But it is very painful for him to observe them. It is like being the father of the possessed boy that he meets many years later. A parent is torn apart with agony at his son's torment. Or the official who pleads with Jesus to come and heal his dying son.

His sinlessness provides Jesus with a terrible clarity about the human situation. He sees what a powerful wound infects the human soul. He sees the self-deception, the lies that we live to protect ourselves from facing our fears. He is not blind to the fact of death as we are.

We have heard the suggestion that it is our fear of death and our need to conceal that unacceptable future from ourselves that drives us to erect massive walls around our psyche to keep the reality of death out. The walls also serve to keep from us the reality of our illusory ways so that we do not even see that we fear death. We can talk about it and plan for it and honestly believe that we are facing it, but it's all a careful fake. When the reality of death breaks in—at a diagnosis of cancer, with its disruption of our schedule, for example—we then experience our true feelings for the first time.

For Jesus death is as fully present as sin is. When he hears a text of Scripture, he is not listening from within a balloon of illusion. His choices draw him ever deeper into the realities of the world and into identifying with these, his brothers, his sisters.

One day as he sits in the class, he hears the prophet Amos:

> Seek good and not evil,
> so that you may live,
> and that the LORD, God of Sabaoth,
> may really be with you
> as you claim he is.
> Hate evil, love good,
> maintain justice at the city gate,
> and it may be that the LORD, God of Sabaoth,
> will take pity on the remnant of Joseph.
> (Amos 5:14–15 JB)

For a typical Jewish boy, certain texts speak of the defeat of the Romans:

> [Your enemies] shall be destroyed
> and brought to nothing,
> those who made war on you.
> For I, the LORD, your God,
> I am holding you by the right hand;
> I tell you, "Do not be afraid. . . . "
> See, I turn you into a threshing sled,
> new, with doubled teeth;
> you shall thresh and crush the mountains.
> (Isa. 41:12–15 JB)

But Jesus is too well aware that the real enemies of his people are not the Romans but the devils who dwell within, keeping them from trusting in the Lord, locking them into selfishness. What good will it be to throw off the Romans if they still do not enjoy inner freedom? What difference does it make to a drunk whether he is in his own home or another's.

Certain texts echo within him as he hears them for the first time. They speak to him so powerfully he will never forget them. One day he first hears,

> "Hear and hear again, but do not understand;
> see and see again, but do not perceive.
> Make the heart of this people gross,
> its ears dull;
> shut its eyes,
> so that it will not see with its eyes,
> hear with its ears,
> understand with its heart,
> and be converted and healed."
> Then I said, "Until when, Lord?"
> He answered:
> "Until towns have been laid waste and deserted . . . "
> (Isa. 6:9–11 JB)

This is his very experience — a people with gross, unperceiving hearts. They are blind and do not see what is most obvious! The words of life are being spoken to them from Scripture, but they are untouched by them, like the deaf. How certain texts ring true!

> The Lord has said:
> "Because this people
> approaches me only in words,
> honors me only with lip service,
> while its heart is far from me . . . " (Isa. 29:13 JB)

How true it is! How it touches him in his lonely awareness, the one sober man amid the drunken with their illusions. The text speaks to him as to no one else. I once heard the suggestion that the Old Testament was written primarily for Jesus to hear. It was to help him in the solitude created by the delusions of others, delusions he did not share. At this deepest level of his self, there is no one to talk it over with. But the texts give him comfort: someone has been there before him—the Lord knew! The Lord knew already the plight of the peoples. This is who God is—the One who knows, who cares, who speaks over and over again of his determination to save this very people, somehow.

> It is the LORD who speaks, and he will carry this out.
> The days are coming now—it is the LORD who speaks—
> when harvest will follow directly after plowing. . . .
> I mean to restore the fortunes of my people Israel. . . .
> (Amos 9:12–14 JB)

What does this have to do with throwing out the Romans! No, it is the devils who possess the people that will be destroyed. The Lord already saw it too, with great clarity. Somehow God will fulfill his promise.

But the evil is so vast and so thoroughly intertwined within the human heart. The people are so unaware of it. They think other people are their enemies; they are unconscious of being possessed by demons.

> The devout have vanished from the land:
> there is not one honest man left.
> All are lurking for blood,
> every man hunting down his brother.
> Their hands are skilled in evil. . . .
> For son insults father,

daughter defies mother,
daughter-in-law defies mother-in-law;
a man's enemies are those of his own household.
(Mic. 7:2–3, 6 JB)

It is so true. At last, a statement of the truth. Jesus never forgets it. It says so well what he is seeing around him. People are so irrational, so self-destructive. They are easily taken over by resentment. How swift are their judgments on others, how automatically they presume well of themselves. How offended they are by anyone suggesting selfishness in their actions. They dwell in a land of illusions. They attribute their troubles to forces outside themselves and are blind to the self-destructive choices they are making.

They are unreal in their approach to death. They take for granted they will live forever. Jesus' experience of people resembles the feelings of the dead in the play *Our Town*. After Emily dies, she is allowed to return to a day in her past, despite the warnings of others. After a few hours of reliving this past life, she flees back to the graveyard. Simon Stimson says to her,

> Yes, now you know. Now you know! That's what it was to be alive. To move about in a cloud of ignorance; to go up and down trampling on the feelings of those . . . of those about you. To spend and waste time as though you had a million years. To be always at the mercy of one self-centered passion, or another. Now you know—that's the happy existence you wanted to go back to. Ignorance and blindness.

She had asked, "Do any human beings ever realize life while they live it—every, every minute?" The stage manager replies, "No. The saints and poets, maybe—they do some."*

Jesus' experience is like that of a saint or a poet—a specific awareness of reality and of the illusion that governs human life. He is both saint and poet, sinless and gifted with a powerful imagina tion, a storyteller of the first rank.

He is also a child and then a young man. He learns about his brothers and sisters day by day, the terrifying nature of their lives.

*Thornton Wilder, *Our Town* (New York: Harper & Row, 1968), 100–101.

9

They are a "crazed species." Yet they belong to him. He does not dissociate himself from them. No, he makes them his own.

I remember a student who would drop in at the headmaster's office each morning and ask, "How's my school doing today?" It was his school, the only school he had, and a school that would be forever his. So too Jesus. He is there and they are there. His life is to be lived out in their presence. They are a part of him. It's rather painful.

But it is a consolation to go to the classroom and hear the word of God. The words ring so true. He walks to the synagogue with a neighbor boy. They enter and take their places. The rabbi taps for attention. "We will take up with Isaiah." Jesus' face turns up, all ears to the rabbi's voice.

> Now go, inscribe this on a tablet,
> write it on a scroll,
> so that it may serve for time to come
> for ever and for ever.
> This is a rebellious people, they are lying children,
> children who will not listen to the LORD's Law.
> To the seers they say, "See nothing!"
> To the prophets, "Do not prophesy the truth to us;
> tell us flattering things; have illusory visions;
> turn aside from the way, leave the path,
> rid us of the Holy One of Israel." (Isa. 30:8–11 NJB)

Now he has words that describe for him the people's strange behavior. Someone has seen it all before him, a prophet whose heart had felt the feelings in God's own heart.

What will be the outcome of such blindness? What is the future for this people? The rabbi reads on.

> So the Holy One of Israel says this,
> "Since you have rejected this word
> and put your trust in fraud and disloyalty
> and rely on these,
> for you this guilt will prove to be
> a breach opening up,
> a bulge at the top of a wall
> which suddenly and all at once comes crashing down.

> He will shatter it like an earthenware pot,
> ruthlessly knocking it to pieces,
> so that of the fragments not one shard can be found
> with which to take up fire from the hearth
> or scoop water from the storage well."
> (Isa. 30:12–14 NJB)

As he walks through the village, Jesus is like a boy whose mother is hospitalized. The boy plays, he laughs even, he enjoys life, he is overwhelmed at times with something beautiful, but his thoughts are never far from her hospital room. Jesus is conscious of the threatening future that awaits his companions, his neighbors.

Later in the week a new text is read as he sits in his place, face upturned, all attention.

> But the LORD is waiting to be gracious to you,
> the Exalted One, to take pity on you,
> for the LORD is a God of fair judgment;
> blessed are all who hope in him. (Isa. 30:18 NJB)

That same powerful stirring of compassion which Jesus feels for this threatened people was already felt in the heart of God, long before Jesus was born. God was already determined to find a way for them. The rabbi's voice:

> Yes, people of Zion, living in Jerusalem,
> you will weep no more.
> He will be gracious to you
> when your cry for help rings out;
> as soon as he hears it, he will answer you.
> When the Lord has given you the bread of suffering
> and the water of distress,
> he who is your teacher will hide no longer,
> and you will see your teacher with your own eyes.
> Your ears will hear these words behind you,
> "This is the way, keep to it." (Isa. 30:19–21 NJB)

> Then moonlight will be bright as sunlight
> and sunlight itself be seven times brighter
> —like the light of seven days in one—

on the day the LORD dresses his people's wound
and heals the scars of the blows they have received.
(Isa. 30:26 NJB)

This is how Jesus comes to know God. God is that Someone
who has already seen things so clearly and who floods the prophet
to the bursting point with his own great love for this threatened
people. What Jesus feels in his own heart is an echo of that great
heart of God, his Father.

Francis of Assisi once heard a Gospel passage read at liturgy
and he knew that Someone had intended this for him to hear, this
very moment! His life was changed. Augustine too. It was just a
child's voice, but when he heard its singsong in a garden nearby, he
knew that Someone Else was saying it at the heart of Augustine's
life.

Jesus finds the Scripture echoing through his consciousness.
Every now and then a text ignites his heart. "That's it! That's
exactly it!"

> Strengthen all weary hands,
> steady all trembling knees
> and say to the faint-hearted,
> "Be strong! Do not be afraid.
> Here is your God,
> vengeance is coming,
> divine retribution;
> he is coming to save you." (Isa. 35:3–4 NJB)

The Scriptures contain all he needs to understand life. In them
is a vivid description of the folly of human life, with its all-
pervasive illusions, its fierce jealousies. They stress the concern of
God and his unbearable pain as he gazes on his chosen ones, and
his determination to save them. This is the world Jesus moves into
more and more as he matures. A boy with his chores and his
classes, his games and his friends; a young man given to endless
discussion of the politics of his village and of the great world;
yet never straying from his characteristic clear-sightedness and
compassion.

He is hearing Scripture as it has never been heard before. At
last Scripture has found its true hearer.

We know exactly where Jesus ends up. He decides to preach. But how he got there we do not know. He has Scripture, his own experience, and prayer as he moves into his dark and hidden future. As he lives from day to day, one question gradually presses on him more and more: What can be done to help this people? This becomes his central concern: How is God to save this people, and what can I do to help them?

He waits a long time. He doesn't search all over the world for his answer. He hears the Scripture and memorizes large parts of it. He doesn't separate himself from people's ordinary life. He observes it and takes part in it. If you lived in Nazareth then and someone asked you who among the young men appeared to be a possible messiah, he would not have led your list. He doesn't lead the discussions, nor does he impress people with his wisdom. He is quite commonplace.

The event is taking place within. The arena is his inner world. He is pondering what to do for this people.

Prayer Exercise

Imagine that you are in Nazareth, a member of a Bible study group. Jesus, the young carpenter, is also in your group. He is about eighteen years old.

Someone is reading a text. Hear the voice, not just the words. Imagine the others, including Jesus, as they listen. After the reading there is a discussion with the rabbi.

Take one verse of Psalm 110, for example. Read it a few times. Then close your eyes and try hearing it. A young man—the rabbi's son—is reading. He stumbles on a word and is corrected. Take it slowly. Waste time.

If the images fade, imagine that a dog or a small child has wandered in, and you get up to take care of it. Afterward you return to the group.

Take the next verse. Read it a few times. Close your eyes and imagine an older woman reading it. Such a beautiful voice! Then the rabbi's voice as he explains something. And so on.

Do not fuss over historical accuracy. Let your imagination do as it pleases. The rabbi's comments can be very simple, not scholarly at all.

The slower the rhythm in which the various images are produced, the more profound the prayer. A willingness to move slowly, to take one's time, to enjoy without rushing ahead—these are signs of a good rhythm.

It's more a matter of getting close to the event than piling up a dizzying sequence of superficial images.

(M. Ballester, *Oración Profunda*)

Let the typical day-to-day experience of the young Jesus and his neighbors fill your imagination. At the end write down what happened and how smoothly the imagining flowed.

Here are some texts for further exercises along the same lines:

Psalm 2
Psalm 23
Dan. 7:9–14
Isa. 40:1–11
Isa. 61:1–4

Chapter Two

As a young man, Jesus visited Jerusalem from time to time. A group would be formed in Nazareth at each big feast. They would travel together to Jerusalem. A crucial incident occurred at the pool of Bethesda during one of these visits. It is recounted in John's Gospel (5:1–14).

Although it is recorded in the Gospel as happening after Jesus' public life began, there are strong reasons to think it occurred earlier. First, Jesus is alone. There are no disciples with him. That is odd. Second, Jesus is able to "disappear" into the crowd, a thing that became impossible in his public life. No one knows him. "The man had no idea who it was." This has led some to suggest that this encounter took place before the public life and was told to the disciples by Jesus. The evangelist then used the story in a different setting.

Here we have a glimpse of Jesus as he lived out the hidden years. He is in Jerusalem for a few days, undoubtedly having come with some others and staying somewhere with them. But this day he is free. There is nothing on the schedule. The group breaks up for a few hours—some to siesta, some to visit relatives. Jesus is left alone. He goes into the streets for a walk.

He doesn't go to the stadium or to the temple. Nor does he go to the theater or the market. He walks to the pool—really a hospital. He encounters the sick. What a peculiar choice. It's not that he knows someone there. He wanders about. He exposes himself to a world of pain.

Do you ever visit a hospital except for your own health or because someone you know is sick? Instead of walking in the park, have you ever just gone walking through the corridors of a hospital?

In Jesus' day you could do just that, and he decides on it one day. "I think I'll go over to the Bethesda pool."

What does he feel as he wanders among the sick? What are his feelings when he sees a man who is blind, another paralyzed?

He starts talking to one man lying on the ground. He finds out that the man has been unable to walk for over thirty years—since before Jesus himself was born. His heart is moved. What must God feel as he gazes at this crippled child of his? Surely God's heart must be filled with compassion for this man who belongs to him. Thirty-eight years of this! The imagination can't tolerate even one day like that, let alone the better part of a lifetime.

Jesus feels drawn by the man's sad plight. He looks into the man's face, listens to his voice.

He becomes sure that God wants the man taken care of. He has no money—no silver or gold—to give him. Besides, no amount of money would deliver him. "Get up!" Jesus tells the man.

What was it like for Jesus to see him get up and walk around? In his early miracles Jesus often hesitates. "Do you believe that I can do this?" Jesus experienced wonder: What can this mean? Is it a sign of what God wants me to be doing—healing? He downplays it. He disappears into the crowd. Later in his ministry he urges silence on the cured. After another spectacular miracle, he flees alone into the mountains.

What could miracle working mean? What do miracles have to do with freeing people from the devils of anger and despair? Has the real problem, the problem of the heart, been affected at all? Because he can now walk around, is the man delivered into any lasting joy? If he can walk, so what? Are those who can walk all that happy? Of course, he will feel good for a while. He will be conscious of how lucky he is. But won't reality be back soon? Won't he eventually get sick again, and die? So what was the healing really about? Jesus' view is clear: Sin is the real evil that threatens the man's life. And so he enjoins him, "Do not sin any more."

All Jesus knows for sure is that the Father's heart must have been filled with compassion for the cripple, a compassion far deeper than Jesus' own, and that God must have wanted the man to walk and to experience the miracle as a call to be healed of the true evil, sin. That's why God had moved Jesus to heal him.

16

Suppose that the man had lost all contact with his family many years before. Suppose that, by chance, his mother—now in her seventies—wanders by the pool and suddenly sees her son lying there paralyzed. When she hears what a life has been his—this son of hers—how her heart aches! It is such emotion that Jesus feels, and it is such emotion that he knows the Father must be feeling.

Despite the tendency of miracles to focus people's attention on superficial problems, still the miracle was God's will. So Jesus feels. But he disappears. He is not yet ready. It is not yet clear to him just what to do. This miracle becomes a factor as he moves toward a decision about his mission. It complicates things for him, as it has done for so many down through the centuries. It would be so much easier intellectually had the miracles never occurred. But they are in the earliest materials on Jesus that we have.

He had to deal with the problem. That the salvation of the people to be worked by God would involve itself with physical cures was not at all obvious to the people of Jesus' day. It was not spelled out unambiguously in the Scriptures. The Baptist worked no miracles and yet he drew huge crowds.

This has to be thought out, reflected on, prayed over, studied. Where is he being led? What is the nature of an effective mission? The miracles and the resultant sensation, the crowds, the exultation—are they a diabolical temptation? Does it make it impossible for the crowds to hear the real message of salvation?

During these years Jesus is constantly preoccupied with the question, What can be done to help this people? Can I do anything that will help? We know that he chose to preach, and that can make it difficult to imagine the days when he does not know. How gradually it comes to him that he is unlike others in some profound way. He becomes aware of an unusual clarity in his approach to reality—an honesty, an ability to see things as they are—that is not present in others. A sense of responsibility comes upon him. He must use his gifts for them.

But this knowledge does not make plain what he should do. What actions will help, what words do they need to hear? There were paths that others had taken. The monks of Qumran. How about that? Is that what he is being called to? Or is he being called to a rabbi's life? He might become a rabbi of such renown that the people would flow into Nazareth to hear him. Or to be a prophet?

For Jesus, during these years of his hidden life, there are two questions. One is, Who am I? What is the significance, if any, of my specific ability to see so clearly into the human heart? But this question is always in the background. In the foreground is the crucial question, What am I to do to help save my people?

He feels a strong sense of mission. People have profound needs, and he has remarkable gifts and a desire to help them. Jesus opens himself to the possibility that God has brought him onto this scene for a particular purpose of his own. God intends to use these gifts for his own kindly purposes. Jesus becomes thoroughly and lastingly convinced of this. Even in the days before he begins his public career, he knows he is being sent. He is being sent by Someone Else, to accomplish the purposes that that Someone Else has in mind. The invitation has come to him in his day-to-day life. He hears it, and he chooses to surrender to it. His life is being pressured by a powerful will, the will of One who would save this people, and who had been engaged in that salvific struggle long before Jesus was born.

As Jesus looks at the world about him, he reacts in a way that he finds echoed the prophets' description of God. That same intensity of involvement that Jesus finds within himself he also finds described in the writings of the prophets. The revulsion he feels, the compassion, the confusion about what to do, the hatred, the love—they are all there in the prophets. His feelings are echoes of God's own feelings.

> Each day I stretched out my hands
> to a rebellious people
> who follow a way which is not good,
> as the fancy takes them;
> a people constantly provoking me to my face.
> (Isa. 65:2–3 NJB)

Yet at the same time,

> past troubles will be forgotten
> and hidden from my eyes.
> For look, I am going to create
> new heavens and a new earth,
> and the past will not be remembered.
> (Isa. 65:16–17 NJB)

The Lord is looking at the people with accuracy. God is seeing them exactly as they are—filled with competitiveness and malice. God knows with precision the dangers they are courting yet is determined to save them. The choice is not based on false optimism. Not at all. God does not see the chosen people as harmless but confused innocents. No. They are rebels, reluctant to enter into the truth. But still God chooses to save them.

There was a veil that veils all peoples and a web that was woven over all nations (Isa. 25:7). Isaiah had seen it so clearly. What consolation comes to Jesus as he sees that his own experience is shared.

Here is an illustration to help us understand his experience of reading Scripture.

You are assigned to a new office. It is so different, and the people are strangers to you. But particularly troublesome is the confusion. The boss is so incompetent. The day is a series of blunders and efforts to correct them. On the way to the bus after work, you hint at this to a fellow worker. But she ignores it. Later you find that nobody will talk about it, nobody will face it. Your experience of utter bedlam can never be expressed.

One day your former boss takes you to lunch. The first thing she says when she meets you in the lobby is "How have you ever survived in that mess?" What a relief! Somebody knows. I can talk about it. I can share my world.

This is Jesus' experience as he reads Scripture. All around him is a web of unreality, and he sees it so clearly, but he has no one to share his perception with. It is so real, so reassuring to hear the words

> "We have made a treaty with Death
> and have struck a pact with Hell.
> When the scourging flood comes over,
> it will not touch us,
> for we have made lies our refuge
> and hidden under falsehood." (Isa. 28:15 NJB)

Isn't this exactly what he is seeing? A people locked in illusion. What is most obvious is never mentioned. They are hoping to live their lives without the thought of death. What a sickness!

> But hail will sweep away the refuge of lies
> and floods wash away the hiding-place;

your treaty with Death will be broken
and your pact with Hell will not hold.
When the scourging flood comes over,
you will be trodden down by it. (Isa. 28:17–18 NJB)

Death will break in and the unprepared will be destroyed.

Throughout his life Jesus stresses the need to face reality. He warns that the great danger is dishonesty, our tendency to fool ourselves when we make our most important choices. How realistic we are when it comes to building a house. We want it built on rock. We consider a man who builds on sand foolish. All that effort and expense and so little return for it. But Jesus sees how we do just that—build our spiritual house on sand. He pictures its overthrow as reality breaks in.

It must have been like watching your widowed mother being persuaded by a con man to invest the family's money in some fraud. Someone you love is being bamboozled and led down a path of promises that haven't a chance of being fulfilled.

Prayer Exercise

Imagine yourself as a citizen of Nazareth. Be yourself as much as you can be—your sex, your age, your occupation. You have come to Jerusalem with a group of friends and neighbors.

This afternoon, after temple prayer, the group breaks up. You and two friends decide to go walking. Let the two be actual people from your life, and let one of them be in a mood that really bothers you. You pass the stadium and the theater and you come to the pool (the hospital).

You are tired. You sit on a bench while the other two walk about. It's hot. You close your eyes. Listen to the murmuring voices. There's a child's voice too. Listen to it. You open your eyes—the crowds of people, the water. Watch for a while.

You hear a familiar voice near you. It's Joseph's son, the carpenter from your village. He is talking to a crippled man. Jesus must be about twenty-two or twenty-three years old now.

Read John 5:1–14 and imagine it. Hear the voices, not just the words, and notice the facial expressions.

At the end write down what happened and how smoothly the images flowed. Write down the answers to these questions: Is my image of Jesus vivid or is it a blur? Is his face taken from a movie or a painting or do I use the face of someone I know? What of his voice? Is it so particular that I could recognize it even with my eyes closed? Or is my focus more on what he is saying?

Chapter Three

The years go by. Jesus is now the village carpenter. The Scriptures are his companion, no one else. When he eventually chooses close followers, not one is from Nazareth. His presence in the community is unassuming and ordinary. He lives buried within the world of first and second and third cousins. The extended family and its joys and griefs sets the rhythm of his everyday life. He can be very much alone in this world, alone and unnoticed. His growth is internal, taking place entirely within him. Even his close friends are unaware of this. He never becomes a figure of importance, a "coming" young man.

His prayer life is evolving. His concern for the people and their needs and his desire to help them are constantly deepening. His question persists: What can I do to help this people? Certain Scripture texts become clothed in great consolation.

> I have made you a covenant of the people
> and light to the nations,
> to open the eyes of the blind,
> to free captives from prison,
> and those who live in darkness from the dungeon.
> (Isa. 42:6–7 NJB)

This is what the people need. It is such consolation to know that God has set his will on it. It will get done.

> See how the former predictions have come true.
> Fresh things I now reveal;
> before they appear I tell you of them. (Isa. 42:9 NJB)

Father John Haughey, in his book *The Conspiracy of God*, tells us that Jesus went from being aware that he was being spoken to, to a time when he became aware that he was being spoken.* We are now at that time when Jesus feels himself invited to see himself in certain texts. He cannot help but see himself in the texts, given his awareness of how different his inner choices are, how unchained, how clear-sighted.

But it is by the joy-filled prayer Jesus experiences that the Father has led him into an awareness of his vocation. At the heart of his inner life—as we see later in his moments of intense religious experience—is the vital text "Here is my servant whom I uphold, my chosen one in whom my soul delights" (Isa. 42:1 NJB).

Jesus experiences God calling him and being delighted with this choice.

> I, the LORD, have called you in saving justice,
> I have grasped you by the hand
> and shaped you. (Isa. 42:6 NJB)

He does not experience being forgiven. God's pleasure in him is unconditioned, pure. God has a task for him. He will be a servant of God.

Servant is a word Jesus uses repeatedly. He finds it a marvelous image for communicating what the good news is all about.

A mysterious powerful will is entering into Jesus' consciousness, a Presence who lets Jesus know that Jesus belongs to him, Jesus is his possession.

> The LORD called me when I was in the womb,
> before my birth he had pronounced my name.
> (Isa. 49:1 NJB)

> He said to me, "Israel you are my servant,
> through whom I shall manifest my glory." (Isa. 49:3 NJB)

> And now the LORD has spoken,
> who formed me in the womb to be his servant,
> to bring Jacob back to him
> and to re-unite Israel to him. (Isa. 49:5 NJB)

---

* "He went from seeing that he was being spoken to, to understanding that he was wholly spoken by the Father." John Haughey, S.J., *The Conspiracy of God* (Garden City, NY: Doubleday, 1973), 36.

This assurance becomes the center of Jesus' inner life. It is being chosen messiah—but with a difference. When we consider the situation that Jesus is in during these years—how his concern for the chosen people is deepening along with a desire that a pathway to safety be opened for them, and how eager he is to let himself and his great gifts be used by them—these texts must have spoken to him, resonating in his consciousness.

By the time he begins his public life, he is very conscious of the importance of his role. From the start he exhibits a strong, unbreakable conviction that he has been singled out by God to play the decisive role in the fate of the chosen people. The vast task of saving this people will get done because the Lord will be at his side every step of way.

> I have formed you and have appointed you
> to be the covenant for a people,
> to restore the land,
> to return ravaged properties,
> to say to prisoners, "Come out,"
> to those who are in darkness, "Show yourselves."
> (Isa. 49:8–9 NJB)

But this gathering assurance of the central role he is to play does not make every step of the way clear. Where does one begin? Should he enter the prisons? Should he shout on the streets? Nazareth? Jerusalem? Today? What should he do?

It is not at all clear just how the messiah will go about his mission. Will he preach? Where? Will he work miracles? Will he become a king? Will he feed the people? How will he get people's attention? Will it be like Moses and the Pharaoh?

Jesus feels it is not yet the time. He waits, alert, receptive, listening. Something is about to happen. When it does happen, he will know. It has not happened yet.

He does nothing to prepare for it in Nazareth. No group of followers is initiated into his secret. He is simply the carpenter. But within, his consciousness is being more and more invaded by assurances from God. At last, God has found one who is perfectly receptive, one whose heart is willing to be formed in the likeness of God's own heart.

That great will of God has found a servant, an ideal servant.

Jesus is undergoing the prophetic experience. He is coming to see the world as the Lord sees it, and to feel toward it as the Lord himself feels. God—within Jesus' human consciousness—is raising up a prophet. Secretly, as the swordsmith in his shop works over a fine sword.

> He made my mouth like a sharp sword,
> he hid me in the shadow of his hand.
> He made me into a sharpened arrow
> and concealed me in his quiver. (Isa. 49:2 NJB)

Throughout his public life Jesus never turns to others for help to know God's will for him. He enters upon his public career full of assurance. His life is founded on the rock of his prayer experiences. He knows God is with him. He knows he has been chosen.

What he does not yet know is when and where and how exactly his mission is to be accomplished.

Prayer Exercise

Use the Bible study group again, picturing yourself in the synagogue in Nazareth, to enter into the small world in which Jesus grew up.

Remember, it is the hidden life. Jesus does not shine. There are no obvious hints of his future. He doesn't appear to be a likely candidate for messiah. He is an ordinary carpenter.

Here are some texts that would be being read:

Amos 5:18–20
Ezek. 12:21–28
Jonah (the whole book)
Mic. 4:1–8; 5:1–5
Hos. 3:5
Jer. 31:31–37
Amos 8:3–11
Deut. 18:15–19

What was his experience as he listened? What were his feelings as he heard the verses on the coming day of gloom and glory? What would have been the feelings of any Jewish child of that village? In many ways Jesus would react as the others did. But how might his reaction differ?

Remember to take it all slowly. Do not try to cover a lot of texts. You are seeking a vivid sense of what it was like to live in his village. If the imagination is not moving, coax it with something easy to picture: a relative of yours knocks on the classroom door, and you must go out and chat with her for a few moments. Even though it appears to be a waste of time, try to imagine this chat vividly. Then return to the group and begin again to listen to the reader.

Chapter Four

Suddenly the routine is broken. Some friends return from Jerusalem breathlessly proclaiming, "A prophet has arisen!" On his next trip to Jerusalem, Jesus goes to see the big event for himself. "Is this it? Are the last days beginning?" He sees John and the great crowds he is attracting by the Jordan River.

What does Jesus think of this new prophet? How does he make up his mind about him? Most of the leaders reject John. He is not authentic. He is another false start. But Jesus recognizes something real. He feels himself accepting the man. Here is a man whose words ring true: the moment has indeed arrived. God is about to break into human history.

John announces the messiah. His coming is imminent, and it will be a time of great violence. How does Jesus feel as he sits with some neighbors from Nazareth and listens to the bold prophet? "Even now the ax is being laid to the root of trees." There's an image. The metal blade sinking into the wood with a crack. "Any tree failing to produce good fruit will be cut down." The crashing of trees great and small is about to happen. They will be cut up and thrown on the fire. Flames will fly toward the sky as the messiah goes to work. What does Jesus think of this image? Is this his own picture of the messiah?

John proclaims, "He will baptize you with fire!" (Matt. 3:11). His words are designed to wake people up. The long night of sleeping is over.

The people love it. They come in droves. They are hungry for this message. In their heart of hearts, they know they need to hear this. How does Jesus feel as he sees the overwhelming response to John? Is he surprised—even delighted? Does he sense it as God drawing them? God is there already, going before John. The soil has been prepared well.

John startles the crowds with yet another arresting image. "His winnowing fan is in his hand" (Matt. 3:12). An arm flies out and the whip rises, and the arm strikes down and the whip lashes at the grain on the floor. Motion, force, violence, and a loud separating of the just from the unjust. "He will clear his threshing floor." It is about to be done. Prepare! "The chaff he will burn in unquenchable fire."

What a clear message! What a strange person! Jesus has to decide whether this is it, here and now the coming of the messiah. The exact script for the messiah's coming has never been written down. Is this wild man from the desert a part of the script? Jesus must decide, and he does. He chooses to believe. He sees in John an invitation from God: out of all human history the hour has come.

What has tipped the scales? Is it John's humility that rings true? He is able to accept an inferior role. There had been self-styled messiahs. But John is not even willing to see himself as Elijah! Just a "voice crying in the wilderness." John has found a description for himself that deflects attention away from himself. That's rare in human history.

Is it the message with its terribly honest picture of the real problems, the sinful heart? There's no hint of the superficial, of the deliverance from Rome's power. Jesus is struck by that. John has a sharp eye for the real problem, unlike many of the leaders.

Perhaps Jesus had already been at Qumran, the monastery on the edge of the Dead Sea. Perhaps he had met John there. And perhaps John had come to know Jesus there. How did it happen? Did Jesus reveal his inner world to John? All through the history of Christian spirituality there has been an emphasis on the importance of spiritual direction, a warning of the risks you run if you keep your inner life a secret. Saint Ignatius Loyola felt that even though you could reach a point where you did not need advice, it was still wise to share your inner thoughts with someone you trust. Did Jesus do this with John? Was this behind John's deference? Did he recognize the authenticity of Jesus' faith experiences, like a good spiritual director might do? Was it clear to him that here was someone of extraordinary holiness? It does happen that way at times. Sometimes in confession the priest can see signs that this penitent is living at a much deeper level of authenticity than is ordinarily the case, even though the penitent is not aware of it. Was Qumran the place where Jesus spent his forty days? It was in the desert, and people went there for retreats. Perhaps there John had come to know Jesus and his great holiness.

John chooses to believe in Jesus. And Jesus chooses to believe in John. John is God's voice speaking to Jesus. The hour has come.

This still leaves many questions for Jesus. "When? Now!" But what to do? How to start? Should he begin with a dramatic miracle? Go to the temple and climb to the top and leap off—and live? At one blow he would have a crowd and a clear sign of his authority.

Maybe he could take a handful of pebbles from the bank of the Jordan and turn them into bread! It would be a wonderful sign of God's love for the people. Jesus has to decide. Suggestions pop into his head as he listens and waits.

Jesus is surprised at the reaction of people. Here at last is someone showing the people the way of uprightness. But the people are behaving rather unpredictably. A tax collector is going down into the water, to the amazement of the crowd. And there are prostitutes listening to every word of John. Astonishing. Even more astonishing and somewhat disturbing is the reaction of the authorities. They come to hear but they do not believe John.

How strange! Those who profess observance of the Law are not attracted by this summons, a summons Jesus feels is right on target. But the religious leaders are "thwarting God's plan for them" (Luke 7:30).

Their response reminds Jesus of a son who is always accommodating to his father in his speech. If he is asked to work in the vineyard, he replies with a gracious smile, "I am on my way, sir." But he never goes (Matt. 21:28–32). The leaders are refusing to be baptized even though it is God's will for them.

While Jesus is sitting there, listening, the suggestion comes to him: Go into the water and be baptized. But he is sinless, and this is a baptism of repentance. It is not only unnecessary, it would be false, misleading. Later in his life he uses the image of kings who never take tolls from their own sons, only from those outside the family. He wanted to show how justified he was to refuse the temple tax. But he paid it anyway, "so that we shall not be the downfall of others" (Matt. 17:26–27).

"True, everything is permissible, but not everything builds people up. Nobody should be looking for selfish advantage, but everybody for everybody else's" (1 Cor. 10:23–24). That's how Paul understood it. "Just as I try to accommodate everybody in everything, not looking for my own advantage, but for the advantage of everybody else, so that they may be saved" (1 Cor. 10:32–33).

It is a profound decision. He gets up and enters the water just like the sinners who need this. He becomes like one of them, his sinful brothers and sisters. He experiences the touch of God, a powerful consolation assuring him that the choice he has made is of God.

There in the river, surrounded by sinners, Jesus experiences God so powerfully—a God coming into the world in power, and sinners welcoming that coming.

During the days that follow, some of John's disciples come to Jesus. He welcomes them, and they become his companions. He begins to form a group of close followers.

It does not have to be this way. He could go on his path without any close followers. It might even help his message. Physical proximity to him was no advantage at all; nothing but doing God's will mattered. Besides, people will tend to interpret Jesus' words by the behavior of his followers. The message might become very blurred.

But he goes ahead anyway and forms a group, an inner circle. He deliberately involves the success of his mission with the freedom of those very ordinary men.

He feels invited to make that choice. God is giving him these men, that is sure. What isn't clear is what to do now.

Prayer Exercise

Take this one step at a time. Imagine each step before reading the next paragraph.

Your pilgrimage group is returning to Nazareth after a festival in Jerusalem. On the way down to Jericho, some friends decided to go hear John the Baptist preach at the Jordan. They invite you to join them. You stay the night at a cousin's house in Jericho.

Early in the morning six of you set out for the Jordan. Already there are others on the road. Everyone is buzzing. There is great anticipation, and none of you has yet been to hear John.

Another road, coming down from the north, intersects yours and the crowds become dense. It is beginning to get warm. One of your friends becomes typically irritable. (Recall a recent irritation from your life.)

As you approach the Jordan you see that the bank of the river is quickly filling up. "I see a good place. Follow me! Hurry!" Your irritated friend falls a bit behind. You drop back and join him or her. Eventually you join the rest.

Look around. Over there are a few wealthy men; a group of Pharisees is nearby; a large group of men and women appear in foreign dress. Some Roman soldiers are watching. Off to your right, closer to the water—isn't that a Nazareth group too? Sure, it's Jesus the carpenter and his cousins.

Suddenly you see John. He has stood up. He begins to preach at once. What a voice!

Read Luke 3:13-17. Hear John's voice, not just the words. Take it slowly, a verse at a time. At the end write down how it went and how vivid it was, how smoothly the imagination flowed.

Chapter Five

Not long after his baptism and the gathering of disciples, Jesus makes a decision. "He went into the Judaean countryside with his disciples and stayed with them there" (John 3:22). He does not head for Galilee, nor does he move into the synagogues to preach. Actually he begins to behave much like the Baptist.

In fact, "he baptized." Jesus baptized! Why? What does he think he is doing? It is not the "baptism with the Holy Spirit." What is it? It was, like John's, a baptism of repentance. We do not have any of his words from this period.

What an odd moment! Is there any painting where Jesus is portrayed as baptizing? Does he feel that this is the path to follow, to be like the Baptist? Later on we get echoes of his resemblance to the Baptist. People say he is the Baptist. Even Herod had heard such a story.

Where does Jesus do this baptizing? In the Judaean countryside (John 3:22), much as John has been doing. For a period of time Jesus is involved in a baptism ministry. Jesus feels drawn to imitate the Baptist. Hearts must be prepared for the imminent coming of God. The Baptist is an effective instrument. Jesus begins his ministry doing the same thing.

Is his preaching the same as the Baptist's preaching with that emphasis on the violent nature of God's in-breaking? We do not know. We don't have a single word.

But Jesus is following a suggestion: Do as he is doing. And he does. It isn't clear what else to do. It seems like a good idea at the time, an effective way of preparing people for the age to come.

But it leads to problems. John's disciples notice that there is now a second center of attraction. They come and tell John that Jesus is baptizing on his own and that everyone is going to him

(John 3:26). What can it mean? It has the appearance of a rivalry between the two. To John's disciples it must look like ingratitude: the new man is competing, and effectively, yet at first he appeared so humble and so willing to get John's blessing. But John assures them that it is no problem.

What a strange moment we have. Two baptizers, each with his own disciples and great crowds. Is the strangeness of this moment, with the many questions it raises, behind the later addition to chapter 4 of the Gospel of John where, in verse 2, someone denies that Jesus was himself baptizing? It is such an odd moment, this earliest public ministry. Jesus appears to be experimenting with a possible form of ministry. He tries it out to see how it fits. It is such a different image from the one we are used to—the Galilean preaching with its many miracles. Here we have a Jesus who is a twin, a clone of the Baptist, no miracles and apparently no strikingly different message, only the baptisms.

Of course, our knowledge of this period is buried deep in the Gospels and is very difficult to piece together.

Now comes another strange moment. Someone tells Jesus that the Pharisees have found out about his very successful baptism ministry. We don't know what he felt, nor even why this piece of news would be of any importance to him, but we know what he decided to do. He decided to leave Judaea and go to Galilee (John 4:1, 3). Why?

And he stops baptizing. Why? He never baptizes again! Yet at the very end he entrusts to his apostles a baptism ministry.

All that we have are decisions of Jesus, and they are very odd. We do not have his thoughts. The Gospels do, though, reveal Jesus as a person who makes decisions and later changes them, a person who is learning more as he goes. He baptizes people because it looks like the effective thing to do. He stops because he sees a more effective path. The correct answers to his questions are not spelled out in detail in Scripture. It is quite clear that God will save the people, and he is sure that his actions will play a decisive role, but just what he is supposed to do from day to day is not clearly indicated.

What if he had chosen to continue baptizing? It would have made a lot of sense. From where Jesus stood, it was a possible future.

But he chooses to stop. He chooses to leave Judaea and to center his mission in Galilee. Why? He chooses to make his preaching the center of his ministry.

Prayer Exercise

As in the previous exercise, read each paragraph and imagine it before reading the next paragraph.

It is a few weeks after your first encounter with John, and now you are very enthusiastic about him. With three friends from Nazareth, you go to the monastery at Qumran to make a week's retreat.

After a day of praying on the edge of the hilltop overlooking the Dead Sea, you gather in a small room with John. You discuss your experiences, and he listens with an occasional comment. Let it come alive in your imagination: the coolness—even chill—of the evening; the great quiet; the candle flame; the faces.

Suddenly there is someone standing in the doorway. A dark figure comes forward into the light. John rises and says, "Jesus, come in!" They both sit. "We were talking together." He begins to introduce us and is quite surprised that we are all from Nazareth.

Jesus is somewhat unkempt and much thinner than you remember him. John asks him about his retreat.

Read Luke 4:1–13. Try to hear Jesus speak the words to this little group.

If you find the images do not flow, let a visitor come, a relative of yours, and you must go and chat for a while. Imagine this conversation vividly. Then try returning to the group and listening to Jesus tell of his days of prayer, fasting, and isolation.

Chapter Six

How does Jesus feel as he hears John's description of the messiah? I remember once being introduced as "a speaker who will knock your socks off." I was surprised. Was that what I was supposed to do? It hadn't said that in the contract.

Does Jesus' image of the messiah fit with John's images? How does Jesus feel as he hears himself described as felling and burning trees, as separating and burning chaff?

When Jesus is well advanced in his preaching ministry, John sends to him some of his disciples with the question, "Are you the one who is to come, or are we to expect someone else?" (Matt. 11:3). John has begun to wonder. Where is the crashing down of the great rotten trees? Where is the fire burning up the chaff? Where is the whip? Why it is not happening as he has foreseen?

John had spelled out a script for Jesus. He is to be like Elijah. That is what the coming of God would mean. Elijah had prayed, "May fire fall from heaven and destroy you!" (1 Kings 18:36–38), and many men died. It is very much a part of the tradition. It is not surprising then that much later in Jesus' public life two of his disciples suggest the same when they encounter resistance. "Lord, do you want us to call down fire from heaven to burn them up?" (Luke 9:53–54). It is the spirit of the Baptist speaking through the two — they had been disciples of the Baptist first, James and John.

Holiness and violence are not kept apart in the images of Scripture. Remember Elisha, the disciple and successor of Elijah. When some small boys persisted in jeering at him, "he cursed them in the name of the Lord. And two bears came out of the forest and savaged forty-two of the boys" (2 Kings 2:24 NBJ).

As Jesus listened to John, was he somewhat uncomfortable with some of the details? When John's messengers come with their question, Jesus responds with what amounts to his own image of the messiah, drawn from other parts of the Scripture than those influencing John's images.

"Go back and tell John what you hear and see: the blind see again and the lame walk, lepers are cleansed, and the deaf hear, the dead are raised to life and the good news is proclaimed to the poor" (Matt. 11:4–5 JB).

He is recalling the prophecy of Isaiah about what would occur on the great day:

> That day the deaf
> will hear the words of the book
> and, delivered from shadow and darkness,
> the eyes of the blind will see.
> The lowly will find ever more joy in the LORD
> and the poorest of people
> will delight in the Holy One of Israel.
> (Isa. 29:18–19 NJB)

Here was a text that had brought joy to Jesus when he first heard it years before at the rabbi's feet. Yes, this is what will be done because God is so concerned about the need of the people. Surely this will be God's way. What desire filled Jesus for the day when this prophecy would come to pass.

Another text that resonated within when he heard it years before was

> Then the eyes of the blind will be opened,
> the ears of the deaf unsealed,
> then the lame will leap like a deer
> and the tongue of the dumb sing for joy. (Isa. 35:5–6 NJB)

This is the script Jesus is drawn to follow. Such a different image from John's. And another:

> He does not cry out or raise his voice,
> his voice is not heard in the street;
> he does not break the crushed reed
> or snuff the faltering wick. (Isa. 42:2–3 NJB)

Where is the ax and the whip and the unquenchable fire? When Jesus begins his preaching in Luke's account, he uses Isaiah to explain himself. It is a text that had been spoken within him years before by God's own voice:

> The spirit of the Lord is on me,
> for he has anointed me
> to bring the good news to the afflicted.
> He has sent me to proclaim liberty to captives,
> sight to the blind,
> to let the oppressed go free,
> to proclaim a year of favour from the Lord.
> (Luke 4:18–19 NJB; cf. Isa. 61:1–2)

That is Jesus' vocation. He is so conscious that Someone Else has made a decision about him, is singling him out for a mission. And this is the call. So he tells John's disciples. And he warns, "and blessed is anyone who does not find me a cause of falling" (Matt. 11:6).

Then Jesus turns to the crowd. He will let the people hear his feelings about John. It is a rare moment. He calls John a prophet, and more than a prophet!

Remember that when John was asked to identify himself, he turned to Isaiah and saw himself as a voice crying out in the desert, "Prepare!" (Matt 3:3). Now as Jesus seeks to identify John, he turns to the prophet Malachi. Malachi hears the Lord speak: "Look, I shall send my messenger to clear a way before me. And suddenly the Lord whom you seek will come to his temple" (Mal. 3:1 NJB).

But it is changed in Jesus' mouth. Instead of God talking of his own coming, now God is speaking to the messiah: "Look, I am going to send my messenger in front of *you* to prepare your way before *you*" (Matt. 11:10 NJB).

Jesus sees John as a messenger preparing the way for the messiah. The role is not very different from the one John had found in Isaiah, but the text is different

Later Jesus uses another text from Malachi to describe John, and here he disagrees flatly with John himself. Elijah had not died. He had been taken up into heaven in a fiery chariot. It is said he will return at the Day of the Lord. So people ask John, when he appears suddenly at the Jordan, "Are you Elijah?" But John says no.

Now Jesus says, yes he is. Again from Malachi: "Look, I shall send you the prophet Elijah before the great and awesome Day of the LORD comes" (Mal. 3:23 NJB).

So Jesus tells the people, "He, if you will believe me, is the Elijah who was to return. Anyone who has ears should listen" (Matt. 11:14–15 NJB). Jesus saw in John, as he listened to him preach on Jordan's banks, the fulfillment of the last prophecy of the last prophet. "All the prophecies of the prophets and the Law were leading towards John" (Matt. 11:13 NJB). Jesus has studied and memorized them. He has seen a direction in them and a thrust. When he hears John, he knows that this is the moment indicated, this is the man foretold. All the anticipation aroused by the prophets' words are aimed at this man and this moment.

Despite his differences with John, Jesus knows that John's appearance is decisive. "Of all children born to women, there has never been anyone greater than John" (Matt. 11:11 NJB). It is a fullness of assurance about John's role.

But Jesus can accept John's loftiness and still reject his messiah script. Even though John cannot understand the true path of the messiah, Jesus does not reject John's true worth. It is a complex judgment. Crucial as his role is, John's vision is limited. He cannot grasp the radical nature of the Kingdom. "The least in the Kingdom is greater than John" (Matt. 11:11 NJB).

Jesus then makes a remark that is quite strange in the light of the contrast between John's images of ax, whip, and fire and the messianic texts of healing and preaching that Jesus has chosen to use. The remark has defied adequate explanation. "The Kingdom of Heaven has been subjected to violence and the violent are taking it by storm" (Matt. 11:12 NJB). An odd conjuncture of John and violence, its meaning hidden.

Jesus might have ignored John. He watched and listened and chose. From our vantage point, it was the obvious, inevitable choice. Perhaps we find any other path inconceivable. But it was not so for Jesus, who chooses each step without the benefit of hindsight. Here is a strange figure, and Jesus chooses to hear John as an invitation from God.

He even launches his career in an imitation of John. It makes sense at first. It seems quite possible that this is the path. It takes a while for Jesus to change his mind, to abandon the baptizing, to go back to Galilee, and to find another pattern.

Prayer Exercise

Take this slowly, a step at a time, as before.

You are at the Jordan. You have been staying with John for several weeks. John is preaching to an immense crowd. Imagine helping people in and out of the river. Be patient. Let the faces of the people be realistic. You are very surprised by someone you know, a rather irreligious person.

After the last people leave for the shore, John and you and one other disciple start up out of the water. This other disciple is a person you find very uncomfortable to be around. Let it be someone from your life.

John sees Jesus and speaks to you. Read John 1:35–39.

You and the other disciple follow Jesus toward the cave where he is staying. Imagine the conversation, a loaf of bread, a dog that pays a visit.

After the imagining is over, write down how it went. Did Jesus notice your lack of enthusiasm for the other person? Did you imagine yourself feeling quite uncomfortable every time the other spoke? Did that person's presence ruin the prayer?

Are you experiencing Jesus as a very strong personality? Is he surprising you at all? Did anything unexpected happen?

Chapter Seven

Jesus poured out images. He said at one point, "I will speak only in images." And his images were superb. They fitted his point perfectly, like the handiwork of a master stonemason. Coming up with apt images involves a whole pattern of creative effort. I notice it in my teaching. A particular point is hard to explain. I realize I need to make it clear. Then (usually in the morning) a perfect image comes, and I know it will work. I enjoy it. And there is more enjoyment when I use it and it works. This experience was common in Jesus' life.

Here is an instance.

Jesus is claiming that he is inaugurating the Kingdom of God. And God is holiness. But something bothers many people as they watch him from day to day. He and his disciples are not big on fasting. All the holiness people around are great at fasting, and they put a stress upon it. They take for granted that anyone who is serious about getting closer to God is going to be fasting. This is still true in our own day. It is really a basic human conviction and it is in all the religions. So people raise this objection with the apostles: How come you people eat and drink freely? How can you expect us to see in you a new path of holiness? John's disciples were great fasters; so are the Pharisees and their disciples.

The apostles mention it to Jesus. What can he say to this? Some suggest to Jesus that fasting might help, but he refuses. He tries to explain why he eats and drinks freely, but they still can't quite see it. How can he help them see it? In a way, how can he spell out his perhaps half-formulated conviction?

With Jesus, unless a teaching finds its way into an image, it is never complete and satisfying. How delighted he is the day it came!

Do you go up to people at a wedding and ask them why they're not fasting? Of course not. So there are common human situations where fasting makes no sense. Great. That's what's going on here. A wedding. Think of these days as a wedding banquet.

But then a better one came. It's strange that it didn't come from the carpenter shop. Did any of his images come from the carpenter shop? All those years at work, but it doesn't seem to be a part of his imagination. This image comes from the vineyard.

When the new vintage comes in, you don't use old wineskins because they will burst from the energy of the new wine. New wine requires new skins. Fasting is an old skin. It cannot contain the new message. The good news cannot be expressed in that pattern. The good news is too different, and to use the old skins would guarantee that it would never be understood.

Another image comes to him one day. It is from a patch on an old cloak. The patch has to be old too. Otherwise the hole gets worse. In some cases you can't mix the new and the old. Fasting and the Kingdom don't mix. The message is too radically new to be expressed that way.

He is delighted when he thinks it up and even more delighted when he uses it and sees how effective it is. What a pleasure for Jesus to overhear one of the apostles using this image in a conversation with a stranger as he tries to explain why this group so centered on God's will and Kingdom do not fast.

Jesus himself had not made a conscious decision not to fast. It had simply never occurred to him to do so. As so often is the case, someone else's criticism reveals to me that I am acting a bit differently. Then I start deciding. Now that I see I am acting so, do I give it up, or do I really want to keep doing this? I feel it's right even though I can't explain it. Often the explanation comes in an image. "Ah! that's why I never felt it important to fast!"

This is something we know about Jesus. He reveled in his imagination. One commentator says that even were he not divine, he would still stand as one of the greatest religious imaginations in human history. We have people like him among us. They do spend time working over problems on the periphery of their consciousness. Like a great advertising genius. She sets up the problem, but then she puts it off to the side. It develops on its own. Suddenly, perhaps in the middle of the night, it forces its way forward. There it is. Jesus has that experience constantly throughout his public life.

He is a communicator. He has things to say. He enjoys saying them well. This was his inner world, a world of image seeking. We have only the end product of all this inner activity, but we must remember all the work that went into producing one of his parables.

Jesus is a man who sees the central part that the imagination plays in human history. He identifies it as the crucial battleground. He does not produce philosophy and argumentation. He strikes at people's imagination. In the world of images, there is no proof, only suggestions, invitations, wonderings. This is where he takes his stand. He raises questions that the people's own hearts will answer.

He was so eager to begin the preaching. Here is a people sitting in great darkness. A light is being flashed into that great darkness. He opens his mouth and reveals things that have been hidden since the foundation of the world.

At first he hopes for a victory in his mission, a conversion of his people. The early days are filled with optimism, the earliest preaching is filled with the great and splendid news.

Prayer Exercise

Use the imagination again, a step at a time.

Back in Nazareth again, you have resumed your ordinary life. Your Bible classes are constantly being sidetracked by talk of John the Baptist. The rabbi feels John is a touch insane. When you tell the class of your strange meetings with Jesus, they are surprised.

On the sabbath a friend stops by to walk with you to the synagogue. Imagine the village streets. She tells you that Jesus is home again. "Maybe he'll be at the service."

As you enter the synagogue you see an unusually large crowd. The only two seats together that are available are next to a person who constantly chats. But you go there and hope.

Join in the singing of the opening psalm. The chatterbox keeps looking toward the front rows. All during the opening prayers the chatterbox is trying to get a better look, stretching left and right, up on tiptoe.

Jesus moves forward and receives the scroll. Read Luke 4:16–22 (don't go on to verse 23). This is Jesus' first visit back home. The people are delighted with his words. Hear his voice. Notice the emotion in his voice as he reads. Can you sense some of the intensity he feels?

Chapter Eight

Commentators suggest that when Jesus first told some of the parables, they had only one point. But when a new situation arose and Jesus needed to explain it, he frequently used an old parable and added a second point. He found that the old parable was most useful for making this new point. In the Gospels we have the later versions. We shall take some of the two-point parables and eliminate the second point. That should help us approach the tone of the early preaching more clearly.

I shall also change the images a bit to give you a chance to hear the parable afresh.

We say that God rules the world; it is his. But different people rule in different ways. What is the way God rules the world? It is like this:

A great king decided to give a banquet for his son's wedding. He sent out invitations to all the royal relatives, especially, of course, the royal aunts (you just don't leave them out). He invited also all the high officials of the kingdom.

But he wanted this banquet to be a very special event. He wanted people to remember it. And he had a mighty big hall. So he sent invitations to all the townspeople and to all the farmers and their families.

Then he went to talk to the chief of the banquet, and he asked him, "Is the banquet hall going to be crowded?"

"Oh, no, sir. There's still room for quite a few more. But we've invited everybody already."

Then the king said, "Go into the alleys and the open roads, and go behind the hedgerows, and get everyone you meet to come. I want my banquet hall full."

There it is. That's what God is up to. With what delight Jesus told this parable. He knew it was a good one. He was to use it many times. It said it all so well.

Jesus had said you cannot pour new wine into old wineskins. But when he turns to parables and images, he does use the old image. God is a king. God is a vineyard owner. God is a shepherd. God is a father. These are old images, the people are accustomed to them.

Now he pours into that old image the new wine—his awareness of what God really is like. Into what appears to be an ordinary parable there comes a character who is strange, unexpected. In what way? He is too good to be true! What king has ever acted like this in all of human history? This is not the way kings behave. Had there ever been such a king even in the human imagination?

Jesus pours the new wine into the old image, and what he had predicted would happen does happen: the image is split and bursts and the wine spills out. The imagination of his audience is jolted. Is this God's true face? The people already believe that God is a king, and a good king, but they do not believe that God is anywhere near this good. This king was so good that he made their old image of God appear to be an idol, a false god. They had underestimated God's goodness. The glorious and splendid kindness of God was not known.

Is it possible that God could be so kind? Jesus does not prove that God is so. He suggests; he invites.

He raises a question: What if God is like this? It boggles the mind. It is intended to. People have to wonder, What if I really don't know God? What if God is very different from what I've believed all these years?

Of course, it produces a certain joy. It's wonderful to hear about such a possibility. Wouldn't it be great?

It's a fine image. Jesus has been able to capture God's intense desire so precisely. "I want my banquet hall full." That's all there is to it. What about protocol? Do you really want to set this kind of precedent? What willfulness! That is the God Jesus believes in—a God who had made a decision, who had set his heart on something. Don't get in his way. "Who will be able to resist the day of his coming?" (Mal. 3:2 NJB).

A forcefulness of will is focusing itself on us. We have fallen by chance into the path of a most determined personality. God has a problem: the banquet hall is too big. (Is this what our lives are lived out within?) God needs warm bodies. The rest will be provided. What is it like to be sleeping behind a hedgerow and to be invited to a royal banquet? It is unexpected—incredible joy.

The people love to hear him. He is preaching as no one has before. It is the real thing, they know it. Where did he get such a corner on reality? Well, wherever he got it, it is the first time they have heard someone preach who knows what he is talking about and who talks about the very basis of human life.

Jesus is delighted at his ability to touch his hearers' imaginations. This is what this people need to deliver them from their dark lives. All their problems go back to that: their false image of God. They have no idea what God is really like. As they come to see the light, and as their hearts become accustomed to it, their lives will change. Once they grasp the great kindness of God, and how blessed it is to be living in his world, their exhausting fears will leave them. They will now have the energies they need to be sensitive to each other. All the energy they lose in useless worry will be saved.

The great day is dawning, the good news about God is being preached at last.

Here is another image that Jesus uses often because of its effectiveness.

The way God rules the world is like this:
There was a rich man who had a wicked son. The son would not work or study, and he spent every cent he could get out of his father. He took to endless drinking and gradually became more and more insolent to his father.

Finally, one night, as all slept, he stole what was in the cash box and fled. He went to a distant town and got involved with sex and drugs. But as the months went by, he ran out of money. He borrowed. He begged. And finally, he robbed. He was caught and arrested. He was offered the choice: a jail term or leave town under escort, so he left that place.

He decided to go back home. Surely his father would not let him starve.

When he was still way down the road, his father saw

him coming. He ran down the street to meet him. He threw his arms around him and kissed him.

He ordered the servants to get a ring and a robe and to kill the fatted calf for his newly found son.

"We must celebrate," he said, "because he is my own son, and he was lost, and now he is found—why, my son was dead and has come back to life."

Again Jesus takes one of their traditional images—God as father. He pours into that image of the good father such a goodness that the image is shaken. One of the commentators imagines the audience listening calmly—until the end. Then incredulity: What did he say? Is he saying that God is indulgent? Doesn't there have to be more to the story than this? Is this young man to be taken back as if nothing has happened? Wouldn't a period of trial be the best thing? Is this really the way to raise the boy? Isn't this indulgent father inviting more trouble? What will prevent the boy from going back to his insolent ways?

Not that it wouldn't be great if God is like this! No, indeed, that would be just wonderful. To be able to start afresh, not to have to carry all my past sinful choices with me. To have that confidence in God's faithful love, a love that lasts and is still there waiting for me when I am ready to turn.

It is such a splendid image of God. This would be another world. God will always be there for us. The people love to hear it. It is a new age dawning. Jesus is delighted. God's true face is beginning to be seen in the world. The light, the truth is entering into the great darkness. Its coming is being greeted with extraordinary enthusiasm.

Prayer Exercise

God comes to us first of all as a word. We hear a promise: "You could be filled with so much more faith than you are." "You could be so much happier than you are." It may appear to be just a suggestion or an idle thought, but it is the Lord.

47

"God loves me." What if I really believed that? God would become my distraction all day long. The thought of God would be always near the surface filling me with a steady joy. Darkness and restless worry would not easily enter my heart.

One way of tasting the great joy of a fuller faith in God is by imagining. Imagine waking up in a world where your mother happens to be God, or your father, or your best friend, someone you trust completely.

At first you would remember the problems heading your way. Then you recall: wait a minute, my mother (father, friend) is in charge of everything. Nothing can go wrong. And even if it does go wrong, so what? What a relaxation!

But the good news is that your mother's love for you is but a shadow of God's love for you. What relaxation and joy would come were you to believe it! That is the joyful day God has in mind for you.

Take a moment to enter God's presence. Ask God to fill your heart with the gift of a much deeper faith. Ask and you shall receive.

Hear Jesus speak to you Matt. 7:7–11 or Luke 11:5–13 or Luke 18:1–8.

Chapter Nine

Yes, it would be so nice to believe in this kind of God—a God of unimaginable goodness. But let's look at the real world. Does it appear to be the creation of such a wonderful creator? What a savage affair human existence is. Harvests fail and children starve. Sickness haunts our days, and death looms so threateningly we cannot even look at it. How can we believe that this nightmare is being cared for by One with loving concern?

Had the preacher of such a beautiful tale never seen a leper and his life-in-death existence? Had he never met someone whose child was possessed by demons? Or a brother unable to walk for most of his life? Or blind, even from birth?

The preaching is beautiful but life is a painful struggle. Could there be—at the bottom of it all—a great giveaway? Not likely. Experience is our teacher. "You don't get something for nothing in this life." This is an adage precisely because it captures our common experience. Whatever life is, it's not a great giveaway. "You get what you pay for." Everything has a price. We have nothing but contempt for those who go through life expecting to be handed everything "on a silver platter." They do not grasp the central law of life.

Now along comes this preacher and says, You are in a world where God is giving away his kingship for the asking. Jesus is not proving this. He is suggesting it in parables. But it seems to fly in the face of overwhelming evidence.

"Evidence!" Jesus began to hear the word over and over again. "Prove it! The evidence all points the other way." It's much easier to believe that God is a stern father. It explains things better. If you obey your father, he helps you to succeed; if you disobey, he punishes. God is like any human father.

Those who are blind? It's because of some sin of theirs, or their parents'. If a building falls on the construction workers, it's because they were leading wicked lives. You can avoid leprosy, but only by avoiding sin.

If Israel rejects the true worship of God, the crops will fail. The presence of the Roman army is a sure sign of a falling away from the true worship of God. That kind of a God makes sense and helps explain why things happen the way they do. When you injure God, he will surely injure you back. The scales must be balanced.

So when Jesus begins to preach this new image, it sparks questions.

What if Jesus had set out on a program of miraculous multiplications of loaves and fish? That would have stifled the criticism. People would not have to work. It would be quite obvious that God had decided to intervene in a powerful way to transform human life. There would be an economic disruption as people enjoyed free food.

Jesus did provide free food once, and the people had no trouble recognizing what it could mean. If you have in your midst a blessed child who can produce electrical energy from his fingertips at will, you have a most valuable possession—the goose that lays golden eggs! A fundamental economic breakthrough is in the offing. With this superb piece of evidence, the miracle of the loaves, the people believe completely. "This is indeed the prophet who is to come into the world" (John 6:14). The new age is dawning, in fact it is present already in this wonderful power.

Jesus senses their conviction. At last he has produced more than wonder and hope. At last the crowd is sure: it is the new age. Is it here that Jesus hears the tempter, "Turn these stones into bread"? Isn't it wonderful to see the enthusiasm of the people for God and for such great kindness? This path of plenty is attractive. But not far down the road, the food will go bad; having free food will become like having free air—no evidence of God's love at all, but just a fact we take for granted each day. Free food, like deliverance from Roman armies, doesn't touch the demons that enslave and torment the human heart. There is a very different gift that God wants to give them, a food that will never go bad. An immortality. A sharing in God's own life. This is the only gift that makes a difference.

But all he does is suggest it, proclaim it. He cannot prove that this gift is available. How does one get people to wager their lives on a suggestion, even if it is of a blessedness so far above physical cures and free food? What dynamic is at work when someone accepts such an incredible teaching? How can the evidence be neutralized? Why will anyone believe an assertion when the evidence is so slim?

Look at the group about Jesus. Is this ragtag collection the herald of the new age?! They look so unimpressive. Is this really the new Sinai? It first came to Jesus personally, in his prayer: Where is the dramatic imagery of the prophecies? How can this scene be the messianic age? He has to find his way into the heart of the problem. His disciples are being bothered by people objecting along this line. "We would like to believe that you are ushering in the new age, but how can we believe when you appear to be such a thoroughly unimportant group?!"

Jesus lets his imagination search. What image will explain the peculiar nature of God's great coming? What is it like?

Perhaps in the ninth chapter of Matthew's Gospel we have the very moment when the logjam breaks, and he discovers the crucial image.

He sees the crowds following him and he experiences sorrow as he looks at them. Sorrow! Ordinarily we do not experience much emotion when we see crowds. During the World Series broadcast, the camera pans the crowds. I am not moved with sorrow at all. But Jesus feels sorrow as he gazes at people. What does he know about them that causes this sorrow?

Jesus feels sorry for them because they are harassed and dejected, like sheep without a shepherd. That's how Jesus sees them: abandoned sheep, confused, milling, looking this way and that in search of someone to guide them. His heart goes out to them.

But in the next moment, Jesus turns and speaks to the disciples using an image of great joy. Where does this joy come from? Certainly not from the scene. Something happened within Jesus' consciousness, something that changes his mood sharply. Is it that image of shepherdless sheep that has seemed so apt to describe the crowds? Does Jesus let that flower within himself? Here is a scene that should depress—the chosen people in such an abandoned state—yet it leads Jesus into great joy.

Jesus wondered himself: What must God be feeling as he watches? God must be feeling a determination to take care of them in their need. God must have seen this and felt sad long before Jesus did. After all, God is the shepherd of Israel. This is his flock. They are not only not abandoned, they are the object of his loving care. God will never abandon them. That would be to go back on his word, his promise.

So God is caring for them already. God doesn't wait until we wake up to others' needs. He goes to work once his ever-alert gaze detects the needs. But it doesn't look it, that's for sure! Yes, the appearances don't reveal God's actions. The appearances are deceptive. He is at work. But it is secret, hidden from our observing. Still, it is God who is at work, and therefore, secret as it may be for now, it is efficacious, and it will be victorious. Don't bet against the triumph of God. Why believe in a God who will lose?

But what would be a good image for this hidden way that God is working in the world? How does one capture something that works — effectively — but without revealing itself? A marvelous image comes, and once again it is not from the carpenter shop.

One day a farmer goes out sowing. His field is not very promising. There are many footpaths that cross it. It is a hangout for neighborhood crows. There are many rocky stretches too. One whole section is covered with thorns. The farmer scatters his seed everywhere.

He goes to bed each night and gets up each morning. The days go by. Through it all, the seed sprouts and grows without his knowing how it happens. The seed produces of itself first the blade, then the ear, finally the ripe wheat in the ear. When the crop is ready — thirty, sixty, a hundredfold — he wields the sickle, for the time is ripe for the harvest.

So it is with the way God rules the world.

Jesus invents an image that he will use over and over again.

Once the farmer chooses to believe in the seed, the appearances are ignored. What difference does it make that the field is so unpromising? The result will be even more spectacular. A person who has never farmed might wonder, seeing nothing happening. For that person appearances are decisive; the evidence is the center of attention. But for one who trusts the power of the seed, appearances are unimportant—in fact the unimpressive appearances are taken for granted.

Jesus looks at the crowd, now through the eyes of trust in God. God is already hard at work among the crowd. God has not waited to begin. He has long been at it. True, it is not apparent. But since it is God who is at work, his victory is already on the way. Jesus turns to his disciples and speaks of the sureness of the coming of the rich harvest. Don't be taken in by appearances. The unimpressive is the very favored scene for God.

But it is all so unlikely. Here Jesus uses an image from the Scriptures to make his point. The construction workers have put aside a few stones to be available for the architect to use in the crucial places—the arches and the cornerstone. Other stones they pile nearby for less important uses. The architect arrives and starts looking through the ones set aside. But he asks, "What's that pile?" They tell him that it's less useful stones. He searches through it. "Don't you have any others?" They had used some—really, broken ones—as fill for a ditch. He must see them. "There it is! That's the one I want!" That is how God works!

The stone that the builders reject becomes the cornerstone. That's how God behaves. Wonderful! Jesus likes that image. It expresses his conviction about God. God prefers to deal with the unlikely. When you experience how unlikely some outcome is, know that God loves that kind of situation.

The field looks most unpromising. Don't forget the power of the seed. Don't be taken in by appearances. God is surely on the move. Nothing is going to be left undone.

Over and over Jesus uses this image. "You must choose. Believe in God's word and not in appearances. Do not seek for evidence—God is working in secret. But it is sure."

All people need is faith.

Notice again how Jesus proves nothing. In fact he reveals why proofs are not central. He suggests the truth as a possibility—"Couldn't it be that God works in the world like a seed in the ground? What if that is the case?" He invites people to believe.

All people have to do is choose to believe. Jesus puts so much time into getting people to identify the really crucial choices of their lives. It is so easy to presume that our choices are unimportant. Jesus is constantly warning that our free choices are critical.

We are going through life presupposing that God is either fully concerned with all our problems or uninterested. What we presuppose is our free choice. We are not forced to live in ignorance. Nor are we forced to believe by all the evidences of providence that surround us. If God is working secretly, the only way to live in the truth is by choosing to believe.

How can you get people to see the choosing that is already taking place in their lives? It's as if everyone is building a house, and some are thinking of building it on sand. What a way to use their freedom. Every word Jesus speaks presupposes that people are free and that their use of freedom is the meaning of their lives. A refusal to believe is catastrophic. The decision to believe is deliverance.

Prayer Exercise

God comes to you as a promise.

God holds out to you a life far happier than the one you live. God made you for this kind of living. The joy that comes from a deep and steady assurance of God's love enables you to open your heart to others and gives you the energy to be sensitive to them. It makes you into a person who is good to have near, not because of the wit you display but the affection for others.

This rocklike confidence in God's love comes to us only as a gift. It is the gift of faith. It is yours for the asking. Enter the Lord's presence and ask for it.

Do you really want this gift? Is it possible that you fear to live at such a deep level of faith?

Do you already live at a very deep level of faith? Is there a gift that would bring you to a much deeper level yet?

What must you do before you get this grace? Do you expect to receive it merely for the asking?

Is God wanting to give this to you? How important is this to God?—that you live today free of the useless worry that exhausts you, in the awareness that all is being taken care of no matter how things may appear.

Is God wanting to give you this now?

Imagine yourself and a few other disciples. Jesus is in the group as you pause under a shade tree. He is speaking quietly. See if you can hear him say, "Don't be afraid: only believe" (Mark 5:36). "When you pray and ask for something, believe that you have received it, and you will be given whatever you ask for" (Mark 11:24).

Matt. 6:25–34 can also be helpful here.

Chapter Ten

In order to explain the peculiar nature of God's way of working in the world, Jesus uses another image. This one comes from the kitchen.

One day a woman decides to bake bread. She takes three measures of flour. Then she takes a tiny bit of yeast and kneads it into the huge mass of flour. When she finishes, she goes off to do her other tasks.

By itself the yeast goes to work, without her knowing how it all happens. Soon the mass of dough begins to rise. Little by little it is completely transformed by the leavening of the yeast.

That is the way God works in the world.

You don't keep returning to the bread and poking it to get it moving. God has a peculiar way of working, and it calls for faith on our part. Go through life filled with trust in God. God has decided to bless you. Rest on that; take that for granted; never act as if it were not true!

Take for granted that God is not out to get something from you. God is out to bless you with gifts. It is strange, incredible, but true. Here is a parable of Jesus put in my own images to give you a chance to hear it afresh.

There is a factory owner in a town where there is not much business. One day he receives a gigantic order. He rushes to the nearest job center to get part-time help. It is nine in the morning, and he hires everyone there. But they aren't enough.

At noon he goes back and gets a few who have arrived late. At four in the afternoon he goes in once more, and he finds some fellows who have slept late that day. He hires them at once and sends them to the factory.

As he sits at his desk around five, the manager comes. "It's done, all done!" They are delighted. He tells the manager, "Listen, give everyone who worked—even the last crowd—a full day's pay."

That's the way God is at work in the world.

Here is a superb parable. What a delight for Jesus when he thinks it up! The image he actually uses is not the factory owner, of course, but the owner of a vineyard. It's an ordinary story, but the ending is a surprise. Jesus takes their traditional image of God, the vineyard owner, and gives it a marvelous twist. A goodness is present, a generosity, that is surprising. God is really working a surprising goodness into our lives, a goodness that is not related to our earning it at all.

Such generosity goes against human nature. It's a law of human nature that we tend to expect as much as we think we are worth. When I work hard, I expect a special thanks. When I am careless and inattentive, I expect nothing special. We are salary oriented. When we put out, we see ourselves as deserving, and our expectations rise. If I neglect my studies and get low grades, I doubt that I'll get a car for my birthday. But if I really apply myself and it's all A's, I feel I deserve something special.

Now, the gift Jesus is proclaiming—the Kingdom of God, his kingship, his kingly activity, his working—has laws of its own also.

It can be given to you only if you know that you do not deserve it. God will not give the Kingdom to you if you think you have purchased it; it is pure gift, a gift beyond any meriting. It comes only to those who see what a pure gift it is, the humble, those who see themselves as hopelessly unworthy of it, who will be astonished when it is offered to them.

Yet—and here's the problem—this gift can only be given to those who do expect to be given it. Unless I have faith when I turn to God, nothing can be given. I must take for granted that God will give it to me when I ask.

Here we have a violation of human nature: a person who knows she does not deserve it at all and yet confidently expects to be given it for the asking. This combination is hard to understand. How can they come together in one person?

In his imagination Jesus sets off to find an image that will help people to understand how these two attitudes can be present together. We can tell how important it was to Jesus by the frequency with which he uses the image once he has found it.

In retrospect it seems a very obvious image, one easy to come upon. It is the child. This image is not easy to hear afresh, we have heard it so often.

Here is just what Jesus is looking for: someone who has no sense of deserving and still has great expectations. The expectations are based entirely on a trust in someone else.

Jesus notices that our actual everyday image of God is not as favorable as our image of ourselves.

> What father among you,
> if his son asked for a fish,
> would hand him a snake?
> Or, if he asked for an egg,
> hand him a scorpion? (Luke 11:11–12 NJB)

The people speak of God as being more perfect than themselves, but they imagine him and deal with him as if he were much less perfect than themselves. "If only I were God, I could relax, I could be secure." Why not assume that God is trustworthy and can be relied upon? It is a choice you make.

> If you, evil as you are,
> know how to give your children what is good,
> how much more will the heavenly Father
> give the Holy Spirit
> to those who ask him! (Luke 11:13 NJB)

There is a note of frustration. He sees it so plainly. They talk about trusting God, but they do not trust him. This refusal to trust darkens their lives with anxiety. Their talking about how they do trust God keeps them from seeing that they lack faith. How can you choose to believe when you think you already believe? The very need to choose to believe is hidden.

The problem is all but insoluble. Because the people do not see themselves as unbelieving, they cannot come to faith. How can people be helped to see that they are not choosing to believe? How can one uncover for them their entrenched lack of expectation?

The child image can be a path. The child does not seek to purchase. He trusts not in his wallet but in his neediness. If he really needs, his father will, of course, respond. The principle is so simple: Ask, and it will be given to you. . . . For everyone who asks receives (Luke 11:9–10 NJB).

Is this what life on this earth is meant to be and can become? A confident request for whatever is needed? The phrase is a defiant challenge: This is what your life can be like. You must choose it to be so. Go through life taking for granted that God will respond to your needs, that God has even more concern than you would, were you God.

Jesus poses to them a criterion by which they can gauge their faith: asking. If their relationship with God is not filled with a confident asking, then they need to start believing for a change.

Jesus imagines what the true believer's life is like. It is filled with such a confidence in God that an instinctive and confident asking is present. Now he imagines what it feels like to believe: "That is why I am telling you not to worry" (Luke 12:22 NJB).

There it is! The constant worry that accompanies people from the moment of waking up in the morning to falling asleep at night—what is it but the outcome of failing to believe. Here is a second way of uncovering your unbelief, by experiencing your anxiety. "There is no need to be afraid: you are worth more than many sparrows" (Luke 12:7 NJB).

Why go through life as if you were not the object of God's loving concern? Why behave as though you must take care of yourself "because if I don't, who will?" "Why, every hair on your head has been counted" (Luke 12:7 NJB).

What a waste it is to struggle under needless anxiety, darkened by groundless fears. The cure is in a person's hands: to choose to believe!

But this choice will never be made unless people see that they do not believe, and, sadly, the depth of their unbelief is concealed from them. They talk of believing. They think it's normal to be filled with worry. The absence of instinctive, confident asking in their lives is just a part of the scenery to them. It doesn't mean they don't believe. No. They honestly feel that they do believe.

In his frustration at this insoluble problem, Jesus even suggests an argument for believing that has nothing to do with whether God is trustworthy. Worry doesn't make sense any way you look at it.

> Can any of you,
> however much you worry,
> add a single cubit to your span of life?
> If a very small thing is beyond your powers,
> why worry about the rest? (Luke 12:25–26 NJB)

Does worry save you from death? That might make worry worthwhile. But since those who worry and those who don't worry die, and at a moment they can't determine, why not live without that worry and its burdens?

His is a view of human life as crippled by illusions that produce fear, and a fear that exhausts. There is an endless need to scramble back to the sheepfold before dark, constantly jostling, pushing, shoving as the light fades. But if they would only stop and stand still, the shepherd would come and carry them home on his shoulders.

It is useless to strive to reach a point where they need nothing. It is their very need of God that summons God's care. All they need is helplessness:

> Anyone who does not welcome the Kingdom of God
> like a little child
> will never enter it. (Luke 18:17 NJB)

Prayer Exercise

As we glimpse the life God is inviting us to, we become aware that we are not yet there. The more clearly we see the life of joy and faith that God intended us for, the farther we feel we are from it. We become dissatisfied. It is a divine dissatisfaction. It is a sharing of God's own dissatisfaction with the unbelief in us, an unbelief that stifles the great things God wishes to accomplish in us.

In ordering you to love God with your whole heart and soul and mind and strength, God is making you a promise: That wholehearted loving will be yours if you ask for it, with desire, with expectation, and with persistence.

Enter God's presence. Bring your dissatisfaction with you. Ask God to fill your heart with an all-consuming love for God. If this is comfortable, stay there peacefully.

If it is distracted or lifeless, ask the Lord a few questions: Lord, do I really want this gift, or am I afraid of it? Is my desire shallow? Am I, Lord, a person of deep desires? Do I have great expectations when I ask? Do you see me as a person of great faith?

The shallowness of your desire may surface. Ask God for a much deeper desire. A great lack of expectation may reveal itself. Ask God for faith.

Asking is for children.

Imagine a small group of disciples and Jesus in their midst speaking quietly. Read Matt. 11:28–30.

Chapter Eleven

Here is an image that Jesus uses on a few occasions. We can follow him as he varies his use of it.

> Which of you,
> with a servant ploughing or minding sheep,
> would say to him when he returned from the fields,
> "Come and have your meal at once"? (Luke 17:7 NJB)

Jesus is letting his imagination play over something that never happens. People are never that concerned about their servants. No, it works more like this:

> Would he not be more likely to say,
> "Get my supper ready;
> fasten your belt and wait on me while I eat and drink.
> You yourself can eat and drink afterwards"? (Luke 17:8 NJB)

"Must he be grateful to the servant for doing what he was told?" (Luke 17:9 NJB). Of course not. There is no call for gratitude. The servant is not doing his master a favor. It's his job.

On this occasion Jesus creates these images to make a very particular point: Do not seek God's gratitude; do not expect it; do not try to do him a favor; do not try to put him in your debt.

> So with you:
> when you have done all you have been told to do,
> say, We are useless servants:
> we have done no more than our duty. (Luke 17:10 NJB)

Jesus elaborates this image to help people understand better how to relate to God. God is seeking not servants but children. Even if you do all you should, you will be at best a useless servant.

On a different occasion Jesus describes a wicked and lazy servant—the fellow who buries his master's money in the ground. But here he has been imagining a useless servant, one who does only what he should.

Jesus is speaking from his experience. He sees servants and masters. He observes the phenomenon. It may have been rather strange from his viewpoint. Even though they are much more tired and much hungrier, servants still serve while the less tired and the less hungry sit at table and eat. How odd. Jesus wonders about that.

He imagines a different scene. "Come and have your meal at once." He tells the people what he has noticed: that they never do that. It is not their way of behaving.

Jesus also notices that they make God into their own image. This is the way their God behaves. He has "thousands upon thousands" waiting on him. God is just like powerful humans, like the kings. This is the way the people see the relationship between God and themselves. That is what they choose to believe.

But Jesus knows that God isn't like that at all.

God has told them, "If I am hungry, I shall not tell you" (Ps. 50:12 NJB). But you do tell your servant when you are hungry. "If I am hungry, I shall *not* tell you, since the world and all it holds is mine" (Ps. 50:12 NJB).

But doesn't God demand sacrifice? Sacrifice easily becomes dangerous by making people think they can win God's gratitude. But they are at best useless servants. "Must he be grateful to the servant?" (Luke 17:9 NJB). Of course not. The psalmist warns Israel: "Let *thanksgiving* be your sacrifice to God" (Ps. 50:14 NJB). But who says thanks, the one who is served or the server? Yet God is expecting thanks! Jesus is entwining gratitude and servanthood into a strange braid. This mind of his is fixed by some crucial truth, and now it is in hot pursuit.

At times Jesus warns people, Death will surprise you. It gives him the opportunity to use the master-and-servant image again.

See that you have your aprons on and your lamps lit. Be like people waiting for their master to return from the wedding feast, ready to open the door as soon as he comes and knocks. Blessed those servants whom the master finds awake when he comes.

I tell you,
he will put on an apron
sit them down at table,
and wait on them. (Luke 12:36–37)

Jesus uses the people's own servant-and-master metaphor. Usually the servant has no power. The powerful go first. God is all powerful. We are God's servants. But Jesus tells them they have it upside down! What should it be? Whoever is most tired and the hungriest eats first. Jesus creates a very different master, and some very embarrassed servants. If people insist on being servants of God, they must be ready to be embarrassed, for their master is going to break the mold. He will sit them at table.

What an image! The new wine is poured into the old skin and it breaks it. How eager he was to preach this new image. How he enjoys watching their reaction.

On another occasion, Jesus raises the question, "For who is the greater: the one at table or the one who serves?" (Luke 22:27 NJB).

Once again Jesus uses the servant image. He really likes it, just as he likes the seed image and the child image. Now he takes the servant image and uses it to suggest a God who is totally strange.

For who is the greater . . . ?
The one at table, surely.
Yet, here am I among you as one who serves.
(Luke 22:27 NJB)

Whoever needs goes first. That's one marvelous way of putting the good news he is bringing. The other god is an idol. God's power is serving the needy. God's wealth is for those who are poor. God's holiness is for sinners. The most powerful has become a servant to the most needy.

From now on if you need little, you will receive little, and if you need a lot, you will receive twenty-four-hour care. Don't put your trust in your deeds for God or your service but in your need of God.

Jesus invites the people to imagine a very different kind of God, a very strange master. When the servant returns after plowing in the field all day, and he is feeling overburdened, and he comes to the master, he is in for a surprise (Matt. 11:28). The master will give him rest. He will put on the apron himself and serve.

Jesus sees God as someone aroused by our great needs, just as Jesus himself experiences this same intense concern for the needs of others. He sees God as moving swiftly to our rescue, like a shepherd seeking a lost sheep. When God sees us needing a servant, needing to be cared for, he turns himself into a servant—out of love for us.

Jesus takes this image one step further: how God transforms himself in accord with our need. When someone we love is sick, we wish that a great doctor, an expert, would come and treat that person. God has such desires also, but he can actually do it. He can become a great doctor.

This image, Doctor God, comes to Jesus in the midst of controversy. People are complaining to the disciples. "You tell us this is the messianic moment, and your master is the great prophet. But we know about holy people. We can read about their lives, and they do not hang about with sinners and the wicked. The psalmist boasts, 'I hate the company of sinners, / I refuse to sit down with the wicked' (Ps. 26:5 NJB), but you people sit and eat with them."

The disciples are puzzled about this. It is a strange way for a prophet to behave. You don't see the Baptist acting this way. It would be so much easier if Jesus would cut back a bit, be more cautious—for the sake of his mission.

Jesus tries to explain why it is important that he associate with sinners, how it is the very kernel of what he is trying to preach. He searches for an image that will help them understand. Then one day it comes.

It is the usual complaint, but this time Jesus happens to overhear it.

> "Why does your master eat with tax-collectors and
> sinners?"
> "It is not the healthy
> who need the doctor,
> but the sick." (Matt. 9:11–12 NJB)

God sees how infected his people are. Death is deep in their bones; anxiety festers in their hearts; malice has them in its grip. So God becomes a doctor. This is why Jesus seeks out the company of sinners. He is God-become-doctor in the world.

God doesn't want you to serve him. He wants to serve you. He wants to become what will be most helpful to you. You are stricken with disease, so God becomes a doctor. You will be close to him if you have a helplessness in your life. Otherwise his service is not welcome. He comes to your helplessness. He seeks those who are overburdened and who are looking for someone to bail them out. God seeks the lost, the abandoned, the children.

Prayer Exercise

God's commands are promises. We are commanded to love God wholeheartedly. This is not a call for massive effort. Nor must we settle for the best we can do, for that will never reach the level of love we are commanded.

There is a promise within the command that only the helpless discover. God has created us to raise us to a level of existence above our own capacity. The power to fulfill the command has to be given to us or it will never be ours.

God commands us to love our neighbor as ourself. We are commanded to love even our enemies. Jesus demands that we love each other as he loves us. These are all promises too.

Jesus tells us, Ask and you shall receive. But we find asking a very uncomfortable way of praying. We experience a certain uselessness when we persist in asking prayer.

The simple asking that Jesus urges on us is not in us. Such repetitious asking is a child's pattern. It presupposes a God who is very concerned and very eager to step in with extra help. Although we may think of God this way, it is not our working image of God, as our unwillingness to keep on asking reveals.

In his word *Ask* is a command and a promise. To fulfill that command we must receive God's help. God's energy must be poured into us if we are ever to come to a childlike asking. We must be brought to birth anew. This is the promise contained in the command to ask. "I shall so fill your heart with the Spirit who will reveal the true fatherly and motherly face of God that asking will become your instinctive way of relating to God."

66

Imagine Jesus speaking to a small group of disciples, a bit apart from the crowd. You are there and so is the one disciple who bothers you the most. He or she is quite unfair to you. Let it be someone from your life who is unfair to you in some way. One of the men asks, "Who is the greatest in the Kingdom of Heaven?" Then read Matt. 18:2–4.

Chapter Twelve

Early in his public career, in the midst of general acclaim and when it appears that his mission is going to succeed, like Jonah among the Ninevites, a rather unpleasant moment occurs.

A young man approaches Jesus and asks him about eternal life. He is a very attractive prospect. As he has done with John and Peter, James and Andrew, and Matthew, Jesus invites the young man to come and share his life. But a strange thing happens. Far from joining Jesus at once, the young man refuses. In fact he is saddened at Jesus' words. In fact he is overcome with sadness (Luke 18:23).

It is an incident that does not follow the script. People are supposed to hear Jesus' words, his invitation, and be filled with joy. But here the most solemn of all the invitations is a cause of sadness. This is not supposed to happen. Jesus wonders what went wrong. Like a poet, Jesus pursues it in his imagination.

How is it supposed to work? How does the choice to follow Jesus come to produce joy? How can a man of great wealth give his wealth up and do it gladly? Why, it happens every day!

> You are living in a lovely neighborhood. A new neighbor has just moved in. As you get to know him, you find out that this is his dream house. For many years he had planned and worked hard to buy it. He spends all his spare time fixing it up.
>
> One day your little girl comes running in. "Mama, Mr. Raymond's house has a For Sale sign in front of it."
>
> You go to the window and look out. A huge sign, obviously handmade: Must Sell by Friday to Highest Bidder. How sad! There must be a death or something awful to explain it. You head over to offer your consolation.

You knock and he calls to enter but he's on the phone and signals you to wait a moment. He's talking to some friend about the sale. He seems happy, in fact very happy!

That is the image Jesus wants. Someone who "goes off in his joy, sells everything he owns" (Matt. 13:44 NJB) in order to get something of much greater value. That's what the Kingdom is like: It is coming upon a treasure hidden in a field or a pearl of great price, and it leads the person who runs into it, the Kingdom, to sell everything he owns, and to do it joyfully.

Mr. Raymond's happiness — even at selling his dream house — is very reasonable. He has come upon something beyond his wildest dreams, an opportunity that comes once in a lifetime, and he is glad to take it. There is a field he walks in and a treasure he trips over, and now his life has only one possible meaning: to buy that field. He loses interest in his dream house. Compared to what he has just found it is rubbish.

This is what it is like to encounter the true God in all God's loving concern. Everything else in one's life becomes unimportant by contrast. Having everything else loses its meaning. What before is precious and important becomes valueless.

But the rich young man has not tripped over any treasure. He is interested in getting more, but he sees nothing worth giving up what he has. It works out so differently when Jesus encounters another rich man later.

This time Jesus invites himself to the man's house for dinner. This is a wonderful event for the senior tax collector, Zacchaeus. He never expected such a marvel. A prophet is going to enter his house and sit at table with him, the sinner! Joy floods his being. In his joy he begins to babble. "Look, sir, I am going to give half my property to the poor" (Luke 19:8 NJB). Jesus just asked him for a meal.

But Zacchaeus has encountered a prophet unlike any he has ever heard of — or imagined. This is surely what God is like. Zacchaeus will never let go of this opportunity. When people start to criticize, Zacchaeus "stood his ground." He is not going to let this joy be taken from him, a joy that is leading him to give away what he treasures.

> And if I have cheated anybody
> I will pay him back
> four times the amount. (Luke 19:8 NJB)

This is how God works. God is not a new task, a new burden, a new step on the way to perfection. God is a spectacular encounter, a marvelous being-forgiven, a deliverance into a new way of living. The joy that comes is liberating. What will I not part with if God sits at the same table with me. Jesus is sitting at Zacchaeus's table, but at a much deeper level of reality, Zacchaeus is now sitting at Jesus' table.

Jesus knew what a joy his command would bring to Zacchaeus. The most powerful has become a servant to the most needy. What happiness is in the heart of Jesus as he brings the good news to this sinner's house. How happy to have this moment, the chance to introduce someone to the true face of God.

On another occasion Jesus puts the same idea in a different image. There is an element of burden, something that we must shoulder, if we are to choose the Kingdom. But hidden to the eye of the one choosing whether to pick it up is a reality that cannot be seen beforehand, that must be taken on trust.

Let's use an example. Your cousin gets you to buy two raffle tickets on a "Bag-o-Gold" prize. You go together to the parish fiesta. You win! As you walk down the aisle, you are hoping, "Make it a big bag!" How sweet it will be if you can't even lift it.

A burden can be sweet. A yoke can be light. But until you pick it up and put it on, you will never know it. It will look too heavy. The rich young man sees only the weight. He is unaware of the sweetness. But with Zacchaeus, Jesus is able to let him experience the sweetness of giving money away.

God and the Kingdom are not a new burden over and above our other problems. Even though the love command is so much loftier than what had gone before, still it is easier. To have to love as Jesus loves can appear too much to ask of us. Not only does Jesus demand such love but he insists that we are not fulfilling the command unless we enjoy doing it. This new insistence on our enjoying it—surely that is too much to ask of us.

We turn the Kingdom into a sheepfold that we must struggle back to and that has now been moved a few miles farther away. It seems to call us to greater effort and courage.

But the sheepfold of the Kingdom that Jesus preaches is much farther away than even that! It is too far away. If we face this fact honestly, it reveals that we are lost sheep. It calls for bleating, not for effort. The fulfillment of the love command is not something God asks of us but something he offers us, something he wants us to ask of him. It is one way Jesus uses to raise our eyes above our own efforts and place them on God's gifts.

A child knows that his father will stand beside him. He knows it instinctively. Once a leper said to Jesus, "Sir, if you want to, you can cure me." Jesus said, "Of course I want to" (Luke 5:12–13 JB). Of course. It is taken for granted by anyone who knows Jesus. How can anyone doubt it? If you are not aware that God is raising your sights to a new and glorious level of life precisely in order to lift you there, you do not really believe at all. You do not know God at all.

Jesus keeps our eyes on that new level of life. Not one particle of the Law is to be overlooked. Its demands are not lessened. But there is a secret hidden away in all that he says. It is a secret known only to children. There is a hidden joy—an inability that leads to being helped, a sinfulness that leads to a loving forgiveness, a lostness that gets carried home. Zacchaeus tastes it, and before Jesus talks of giving "all you have to the poor," Zacchaeus begins to give it away.

But to the rich young man who does not taste it, it is all rather depressing.

Prayer Exercise

Take it a paragraph at a time.

You are now a close follower of Jesus. Last night the band of disciples divided up. You and three others are in the house of a cousin of Thomas in Capernaum. You wake up in a strange room.

Let your present mood surface. There is a knock on your door. "Let's get coffee." It is a close friend, who is also an apostle. You both go to the kitchen.

There you find another apostle already sitting at the table. This is a person whom you would rather not meet. Let it be someone from your life. A typical friction occurs. Imagine it vividly and carefully. At the worst possible moment for you, Jesus walks in looking for a cup of coffee. He reacts. Others drift in. Everyone is chatting.

Jesus says, "Today I shall preach on the hillside." You head out with some others.

When you reach the hillside there are huge crowds. They quiet down as Jesus stands to speak. Read Matt. 13:44–50.

Hear his voice. Notice that the disciple who bothers you is sitting rather close to Jesus and is totally absorbed in listening.

Jesus preached the Kingdom of Heaven. To understand the joy that comes with entering the Kingdom, we must be realistic. The apostles did not become saints the day they met Jesus. In imagining the life of Jesus, we easily fall into the error of picturing him surrounded by a loving band of saints. They were a highly competitive group.

If I imagine myself as a disciple who loves all the other followers of Jesus, I falsify Jesus' reality. It wasn't his experience at all. He was surrounded by human competitiveness. His good news was for them, not for the holy ones. God's Kingdom is aimed at people who are angry and impatient, jealous and resentful.

You do not have to stop being unloving in order to receive God's help. The help must come to you first, and only that help will free you from inability to love.

In imagining myself as a close follower of Jesus, I must include in the picture my own wounds, my inability to love some people, my indifference to some, my angers and resentments. Then I will hear Jesus' words in a very different way. Each word will be meant for me, not just for the others who need to hear this.

Just as there are constant frictions in our daily lives, so too among Jesus' followers there were problems. We must include them in our imagining even if it "ruins" our prayer.

Chapter Thirteen

It is interesting to notice how Jesus responds to dramatic news. "The Pharisees know you are baptizing." "Herod is out to get you." Here is another incident.

> When Jesus received this news
> he withdrew by boat to a lonely place
> where they could be by themselves.
> (Matt. 14:13 NJB)

Jesus wants to get away. He needs time to reflect and pray. What news is being told to him? The Baptist has been put to death. It means something to Jesus, and he has to work it out. What does it mean for his mission?

The news brings to Jesus' mind a pattern that has begun to appear in his own ministry. It brings a lot of incidents together and causes him to wonder about the real thrust beneath them.

Earlier he had made a similar decision—he had withdrawn from one district. He had entered the local synagogue and worked a spectacular cure. It was the sabbath and he knew that his cures on the sabbath were creating a problem for some. It seemed to them a violation of the sabbath observance. Before he cured the withered hand, he found an image he thought would help people to understand. If they can grasp what is behind the cure, they might suddenly get a sense of the great news he is preaching.

He told this story:

> A man has only a single sheep. He leaves it in the care of his young son. But one day the sheep nibbles too near the edge of the cliff and slips and now is caught part way down. The boy hurries to his father. On his way he runs into the rabbi, who calls him to him.
>
> "Why are you running on the sabbath, Aaron?"

He tells the rabbi of the sheep and how it is in danger.
They both get the father and all three lift the sheep to safety.

"Now, a man is far more important than a sheep."
(Matt. 12:12 NJB)

Then Jesus asked the crowd, "Is it permitted on the Sabbath day to do good?" (Mark 3:4 NJB). But nobody spoke. They just sat silent. Jesus was shocked by this, and saddened. How could they refuse to see it? They are not going to give in.

Not giving in is a rather human way of behaving. We refuse to give in even after the battle is lost. We refuse to admit we are wrong even when the evidence is staring us in the face. It is frustrating to deal with that mentality.

When the Pharisees left together without any friendly gesture toward Jesus, he knew their hostility. And he himself made the decision to leave that district.

So too now at the news of the Baptist's death. Jesus decides to get away. In this instance it doesn't work, for the crowds follow, but eventually Jesus does find ways of getting apart. He even leaves Israel on one occasion, so eager is he to be by himself and to think it all through.

So the Baptist is dead. The Elijah has come and they do not recognize him. Unbelievable. They have "treated him as they pleased" (Matt. 17:12 NJB). Who would have ever imagined it could happen—the Elijah being put to death. What kind of Day of the Lord is approaching? An Elijah rendered helpless, having his head cut off! So different from the powerful Elijah of the past. And this is the introduction to the messianic age. What strange form will it take if this unexpected event was its preparation?

If the Elijah figure meets death, what of the messiah figure? Is it possible that John's career is meant to help Jesus shift gears into the hidden reality of the messianic age? A horror is approaching: the messiah will be put to death by the chosen people! What an image. It is in Jesus' imagination that this horrible image is first formed.

During these days, alone with his disciples, Jesus begins to search for God's will for him. What will help this people if his preaching is not going to convert them?

It is so clear now as he looks back. His experiences at Nazareth had been typical. He was welcomed when first he preached at Nazareth. "They were astonished by the gracious words that came from his lips" (Luke 4:22 NJB). But later on he was unable to work any miracles there. People had no faith in him and his preaching. On his latest visit, the people became angry at him and hustled him out of town (Luke 4:29).

At his coming many are delighted but others are enraged. An invitation to a banquet is producing only anger in some. Why? How can this happen? How can people reject an invitation to a banquet? How can the truth be preached and meet rejection? How can God's true face be revealed and people see it and turn away? How can it be that such kindness, hidden since the foundation of the world, is revealed and yet not convert the hearers?

What frustration! His hopes are dashed. It is so unexpected. It is somehow connected to the fact that he is preaching to the chosen people. This is the strangest element for Jesus to grapple with. As he thinks of it, he feels that had he gone to the pagans and preached among them, they would have believed. It is precisely this: The chosen people are to reject their messiah.

We see it so clearly in retrospect, and it looks so obvious to us. But Jesus is putting it together for the first time, and it is strange beyond belief. It is only by entering into his experience that we can grasp the upsetting of all expectations that is at the heart of his mission.

Often when we are deeply committed along a particular path and things begin to go sour and fail, we daydream: What if I had gone to medical school instead? What if I had accepted that scholarship in Colorado instead of staying here? We picture ourselves in our daydream as being so much more successful.

Jesus does the same. His mission is going sour. His high hopes are confronting a brutal reality. He wonders, What would have happened if I had gone to work among the pagans instead of among the chosen?

Why did he choose to imagine such a strange scenario? Had Jesus ever wondered, as he prayed his way to a career decision, on the possibility of going among the pagans? I doubt it. But then where does he get this image?

Perhaps the words he uses to flesh out his daydream will reveal where it came from. He imagines a mission to the pagans of Tyre and Sidon. He sees himself a marvelous success. What are the images of success for Jesus? Great crowds? Many miracles? A theocratic state? A palm procession? No, the signs of success in his image are sackcloth and ashes. Now, these are not the usual images we employ for success. Were I to imagine a highly successful priestly career, I would never think of sackcloth and ashes as a part of it. Where Jesus does have success, nobody puts on sackcloth and ashes anyway. Why does he choose these terms?

I think he gets it from a scriptural image that grips him powerfully. A great city is in trouble and facing destruction. God looks down and in his compassion decides to save the people. God sees that preaching will be all that is needed. So God chooses a preacher. It works. The people listen, even the leaders. It is, as you may have guessed, the Book of Jonah.

This is an image Jesus likes a lot. It is a close parallel to his own situation. There is a people heading for destruction and a very concerned God. Jesus feels God call him to preach to this people. He preaches, but there the resemblance ends. Something goes wrong with the script he is following.

But how can it go wrong? After all, Jonah had a tougher audience—the pagans. Jesus has all the odds in his favor. If it works for Jonah with the hostile, unbelieving Ninevites, how much more will Jesus' succeed with the chosen people.

Jesus preaches and the people hear the preaching and demand signs. Signs! They are hearing the truth. What do they need signs for? Do the Ninevites say to Jonah, "Give us a sign!"? Of course not. It is a surprise when Jesus hears people asking for signs, a very unpleasant surprise. Why, what sign does Jonah give the people of Nineveh? All they see is a hated Jew walking their streets and preaching this very unwelcome message. But that was enough for them.

> "It is an evil and unfaithful generation
> that asks for a sign.
> And the only sign it will be given
> is the sign of Jonah."
> And he left them and went off. (Matt. 16:4 NJB)

76

He is surprised and grieved at their resistance. And he is angry at them. He vividly sketches the day of judgment: "The people of Nineveh will appear against this generation" (Luke 11:32 NJB). Two generations will stand facing each other—a pagan one and a Jewish one, the very special generation chosen to hear the messiah. The pagan one will condemn the chosen one

> because when Jonah preached
> they repented,
> and, look,
> there is something greater than Jonah here. (Luke 11:32 NJB)

It is in the Book of Jonah that the images of Jonah's success were sackcloth and ashes. That is how the author describes what the people did in responding to Jonah's preaching. That is where Jesus gets these images of success. During the earlier, successful period of his ministry, the Jonah parallel was always in the back of his mind. When the reality begins to diverge from the script of the Jonah story, Jesus becomes explicit:

> Alas for you, Bethsaida!
> If the miracles done in you
> had been done in Tyre and Sidon,
> they would have repented long ago
> in sackcloth and ashes. (Matt. 11:21 NJB)

Jesus has imagined a different scenario, a successful one. "What if I had gone to the pagans?" "If only I had gone into medicine instead."

Prayer Exercises

Saint Augustine tells us in his *Enchiridion* (117) that the crucial moment in the decision to believe occurs when you believe in this: "that the power to love will be given to you when you ask for it."

But what if I already do love. Like the rich young man who met Jesus, I can say, "I am a loving person." Then I am quite blind to my real story.

Here are two exercises that can help uncover hidden levels of lack of love.

First Exercise

Picture a room, two chairs, a movie screen. You sit in one chair and the heavenly Father sits in the other. The room lights go out. The screen lights up.

It is a film about you. You are in an act of resentment. Let it be an everyday act, not something far back in the past. Let it be a single act, not a series. Let it be the kind of uncharity you have a history of.

Watch yourself on the screen for three or four minutes.

Then the screen goes dark.

Ask yourself, How did I feel as I watched myself? How did the Father feel as he watched me?

Then read Matt. 18:23–35, a parable in which Jesus suggests the Father's feelings.

Second Exercise

Imagine yourself in an act of uncharitableness.

Notice all the gifts you use in order to perform that act: being, life, eyes, intelligence, tongue, will, legs, breath, voice.

Imagine the Father watching you as you use his (love's) gifts to be unloving. How does the Father feel?

Read Ezekiel 16, a prophet's parable on how the Father must feel.

If the imagination moves slowly, the images will be so vivid that much of the original emotion will return from the depths where it lies hidden. It is a most unpleasant sight—the angry me, the very resentful me. It is painful to experience and the impulse to stop it is strong. But the gospel invites us into this very real part of ourselves.

It is only by growing in the truth about myself that I encounter the true Jesus, not an idol of my own making.

Chapter Fourteen

Besides daydreaming about success when we are confronted with failure, we also tend to search for the reasons why we have failed. Jesus does this too. He tries to discover the deepest levels of this resistance to the gospel.

One reason for the opposition is very obvious: the human refusal to face the fact of death. To promise someone that you will stand by them at the great judgment is to remind them that they will indeed be judged. This reminder may be so unwelcome that the good news becomes also unwelcome. "I will raise you up" can be very threatening because it implies that you will die. "I will raise you up from death."

It's like arriving home from vacation and being met at the airport by your boss with the good news, "Don't worry, we're going to bail you out and get you the best lawyer money can buy!" You didn't even know you were up on charges.

So at the very heart of the good news—the promise of the resurrection—is a reminder that we will die. But we prefer to live as if life lasts forever. We vigorously resist anything that threatens to make the fact of death come alive in our consciousness. We live in the darkness of this illusion, determined not to be exposed to this light.

But Jesus searches for the ultimate source of resistance. We can follow his searching in his parables. His glorious message of the unexpected goodness of God meets an unexpected reception. Why is the messianic age being greeted with determined hostility? It isn't just this person or that person. It is something more ominous than that. It is a rude awakening for Jesus to discover that, yes, there is someone simply determined not to like him or his preaching.

He tries to capture that moment of surprise in a parable. He uses an image he has used earlier, and he puts into it the new experience.

> A sower went out and sowed his field, all his hired hands helping him until it was done. While everybody was asleep, the seed began to grow of itself. One night along came a man who sowed darnel all among the wheat and made off.
>
> When the new wheat sprouted and ripened, the darnel appeared as well. His workers went to the man and said, "Was it really just wheat that you sowed in your field? Was it good seed?"
>
> "Yes, indeed, it was."
>
> "Then where does the darnel come from?" they asked him.

This is the question facing Jesus. Where is this unexpected resistance coming from? The harvest is going to be great, but a problem has arisen.

Then the man told the laborers, "An enemy has done this" (Matt. 13:24–28a).

Just as Jesus is now seeing it, so too does he become aware that God has seen it before. Once again he chooses to believe in a God who has already been introduced to this enemy. Now Jesus comes to know: God has an enemy. That enemy is set on preventing the success of Jesus' mission. That enemy must make sure that this people not be delivered from the destruction that threatens them, that they be blinded and led in the dark away from the good news, that they be deafened.

How does one get inside the human heart and make it reject this splendid invitation? Where is a door into the soul by which this enemy can enter?

Jesus now searches for the heart of the resistance to his preaching. When he discovers it, he will compare it to a yeast because its beginnings are so hidden. It is so harmless in its appearance that it is welcomed in. It doesn't look dangerous at all. Jesus will isolate it and warn his followers about it. He will carefully reveal its apparently innocuous symptoms. It is dangerous.

Keep your eyes open,
and be on your guard
against the yeast. (Matt. 16:6 NJB)

What is this harmless-looking source of such a mortal infection? Once Jesus finds it, he puts it in parables. But he uses the parables he has already used. It is the banquet, because the man has found his son again. Yes, he is a wicked son, as ungrateful and selfish as he can be. But now he is back, and there has to be a great rejoicing. This is the way God rules the world. He invades the human story as a free forgiveness:

. . . to give them for ashes a garland,
for mourning-dress, the oil of gladness,
for despondency, festal attire. (Isa. 61:3 NJB)

Here Jesus introduces another surprise. There is an elder brother. In this brilliantly imagined person, Jesus explains why an invitation to a banquet can be a cause of great pain. When the elder brother hears of the banquet "he was angry and refused to go in" (Luke 15:28 NJB).

This is what Jesus encounters—anger at his invitation. When the father comes out to urge him to come in, the brother points out the injustice of the father's decision to forgive. It is not fair!

We can sympathize with this feeling. After all, God wants us to cooperate, yet whether we choose to cooperate or not, God treats us the same. God has placed in us a sense of fairness, and yet he himself violates it.

On another occasion Jesus swiftly produces an image that puts this same point quite well and leaves his hearer baffled at the radical nature of God's new covenant. It is at the Pharisee Simon's house. A prostitute enters and weeps at Jesus' feet and he is moved to forgive her sins.

To help Simon see what this new age is like Jesus invents a marvelous image.

There once was a money-lender. Among his many clients, there were two men who were unable to pay him back. He decided to let them both off.

Now one of them owed him five hundred denarii, and the other only fifty.

Which of the two will love him more?

And Simon has no trouble finding the answer: "The one who was let off more, I suppose" (Luke 7:43 NJB). Jesus is introducing Simon to a new way of relating to God. "It is someone who is forgiven little who shows little love" (Luke 7:47 NJB).

It doesn't seem fair. You try to do your best. As a result you have little to be forgiven, and it turns out that that results in loving God less! It sounds like an invitation to sin. "Shall we persist in sin, so that there may be all the more grace?" (Rom. 6:1). It seems to be suggesting that.

Jesus is attacking Simon's grading system. In it Simon gets an A while the prostitute is failing. But the Scriptures have warned Simon already—Not so!

> The LORD looks down from heaven
> at the children of Adam.
> To see if a single one is wise,
> a single one seeks God.
> All have turned away,
> all alike turned sour,
> not one of them does right,
> not a single one. (Ps. 14:2–3 NJB)

Simon is wrapped in illusion. The sense of well-being that he experiences from his image of himself as a person who basically cooperates with God and tries to do his best—this sense of spiritual well-being is based on keeping his eyes closed. It can be cured only by opening his eyes.

Another image that Jesus employs seems to be an invitation to say no to God.

> A man notices that the lawn has not been cut in three weeks. He finds his son and asks him to do it. The boy replies, "Gladly, Father. I will be happy to do it." But he doesn't.
>
> Later when the man notices that the grass is still uncut, he runs into his other son, and he asks him, "Would you cut the grass?" But the boy replies, "No, I won't. The other boy is supposed to do it." And he walks away angry.

But soon he feels bad at how he had spoken to his father and he goes out and mows the lawn.

Jesus notices the way we behave. He sees how the nicest words so often accompany a rejection. Humans have discovered a gap between their hearts and their mouths. It can be very useful. The mouth can be used to deceive others about what is in the heart. But, unfortunately, the mouth can also end up deceiving the self about what is in the heart. When that happens, you live unaware of your own real heart, and that is to live in darkness.

Isn't this the case of the rich young man? He reaches such a sense of spiritual wealth that he sees himself as fulfilling all the commandments — even the love command (Matt. 19:19). What has Jesus to offer him? But Zacchaeus knows — thanks to the constant preaching of the rabbis — that he is a sinner.

Jesus imagines the prayer of those who have a strong sense of their spiritual wealth. It is a prayer filled with thanksgiving. "Thank you, Lord." He contrasts it with the request for mercy that is true prayer. But requesting mercy is a prayer that makes no sense to those who judge themselves to be doing their best.

Simon has to learn honesty, a ruthless honesty about himself that will lead to the exultation of being forgiven. The elder brother is convinced that the basic rules of fairness are being violated. His image of himself is filled with an illusion that guarantees a rejection of the gospel:

> All these years I have slaved for
> you and never once disobeyed any
> order of yours. (Luke 15:29 NJB)

What a satisfying self-image. What an offensive image of his father — the slave-master! How well Jesus feels his way into the sense of injustice that the young man is experiencing. His words are so vivid that we sympathize with this selfishness! It is our own salary mentality that is embodied, our instinct for dealing with God as with a slave-master.

Jesus has the father gently correct the son's description of their life together. It has not been a slavery but a family. "You have been with me all these years." Wasn't that a joy? You began a son; how did you end up a slave?

This parable, which served Jesus well when he wished to reveal the good news of God's unexpected goodness, now is used to help locate the real source of resistance to the gospel. Enmity to God gains entry into the human soul and is welcomed because it offers a very pleasing self-image in place of the truth. It attaches all the promises of reward to this pleasing self-image and detaches them from those who are seen as short of that same mark.

The need to be forgiven is not part of the package. The elder brother with his careful accounting of all he has done and his acute awareness of what is due to him can only find the banquet a joke. He cannot go in. It would be too painful to have to sit and watch as forgiveness takes center stage. He will be happier spending the night in the barn. The banquet would be an agony. It is an image of a person who does not want to enter heaven. The banquet would be too unbearable because it would call upon him to reevalute his life. What he sees as deserving reward—his own life—would have to be seen as needing forgiveness.

Jesus has introduced this figure of unexpected malice into a parable of unexpected goodness.

Why is the gospel being rejected? Because it is being offered to everyone. In other words, precisely because it is such a spectacular goodness. I have created a view of the world that requires that God not do too much kindness. To me or anybody. To me, because I don't need it. I can pay my way (thank God!). But if all are to be forgiven, then paying my way means nothing.

Into Jesus' experience of preaching the unbelievable kindness of God another experience comes—rejection. This field, sure to give a great harvest, is growing more than wheat. Just as God is at work among those who listen, preparing them to recognize the truth of the good news Jesus will preach, so too another force is at work.

Secretly, into the human heart, an enemy enters. The path he follows is a remembering and a forgetting that give pleasure. He gets people to be very conscious of the good they do, to remember it, to store it up like a treasure. He also gets them to notice (How can you fail to notice? Are we supposed to become blind to reality?) whenever others are at fault. It produces a pleasant image of the self.

Its working is secret and instinctive. The pleasure it produces becomes vital to day-to-day living. It means that I lose accurate self-knowledge. I have learned how to forget my faults, my unloving ways, my reluctance to trust God. I see myself as a basically cooperative person, not perfect but doing the best I can. At least trying.

Once I lose an accurate knowledge of what is in my heart, without being aware that I have lost it, I can say yes and intend no. "Of course, Father, I will go and do it gladly." I can say I love someone and actually feel I do, and all the while my real hatred is known only to others.

Jesus discovers the cause of the rejection. He also locates the antidote. Be honest. If there is a no in the heart, let there be a no on your lips—even to God! It is the lie that destroys all chance of dialogue. What if the elder brother had pretended he was happy and entered the banquet? The dialogue would never have occurred—a dialogue in which his father gets a chance to invite him to more than a banquet, to invite him back into the truth about himself. It is only if he is willing to hear of his own great need to be forgiven for leading a life so self-centered that he will be able to enjoy the banquet.

Jesus meets people who find his God of unexpected goodness repulsive. They are so angry at this wave of forgiveness that they want it halted. Any weapon must be used. "Show us a sign from Heaven!"

> "This is an evil and unfaithful generation
> asking for a sign,
> and the only sign it will be given
> is the sign of Jonah."
> And he left them and went off. (Matt. 16:4 NJB)

His preaching is in ruins. What should he do?

Prayer Exercise

Take this a step at a time. Don't read ahead.

Martha and you are the only ones at home when lunchtime comes. You no sooner have everything ready to eat when Jesus comes in talking with Peter. Two extra mouths. But Peter has to leave. The three of you sit and chat.

Martha remarks how tired Jesus looks. "But I'm really very happy today." She asks why. Jesus tells you both of his experience with this non-Jew, a centurion, a man who believed so simply in Jesus' power and goodwill: "Never among all the Jews in Israel have I met a man with faith like that!"

You say, "I wish I had faith like that." Jesus looks at you:

"Ask, and keep on asking!"

"If your nephew asks for bread,
do you give him a stone?"

"Don't you realize
that your heavenly Father will do as much?"

It seems so simple. Martha tells about her homework for the rabbi's class. She must tell the class her favorite Scripture verse. She has chosen Psalm 23, "The Lord is my shepherd."

There is some joking among the three of you, and then Jesus asks, "What is my favorite passage, can you guess?"

You let Martha try first.

Then you guess.

Finally Jesus says, "Here it is: 'You shall love the LORD your God with all your heart, with all your soul, with all your mind, and with all your strength.'"

You say, "I wish I loved God like that." Jesus says:

Listen to me. Ask and you shall receive! If you trust me, you will be like a person who builds a house on a strong foundation laid upon the underlying rock. You will stand firm when the storms come.

Enter the presence of God, and ask for the gift to know Jesus more, to love him more, and to follow him more closely.

Chapter Fifteen

What is it like to be Jesus? What choices does he have? What can he do other than what he did? We must look at the things he chooses not to do or we will never grasp his inner experience.

The central choices of Jesus' life, those choices that most make him himself, are in the area of faith. A faith choice is a decision to trust somebody amid circumstances that neither dictate this trust nor rule it out. The evidences are such that they do not settle the question of trustworthiness one way or the other. In such a situation it is reasonable to trust and it is reasonable not to trust. Reasonable people can do either.

The decision to trust in such a moment comes not from the head but from the person's freedom.

To get inside Jesus' consciousness and see the particular nature of his inner experience, let us use an image to illustrate the free choices to trust that we make.

> George and I have been good friends since the fifth grade. He is at college in New York, but whenever he's in town, we play racquetball and go to dinner. He tells me he's coming to Washington for two weeks at Christmas and will be at his parents' house.
>
> Christmas comes and the days go by and I don't hear from him. I would call, but he doesn't want me to call his parents' house. I may start to wonder. Has he forgotten me? Have new friends come along and made me part of the past? But the thought comes: He has probably not been able to get to town. He'll be calling me from New York to tell me what went wrong. I choose to believe that and I'm at peace. George would never desert me.

On New Year's Eve I run into Sally. She tells me she saw George with his parents at midnight Mass and he looked fine. Well! What's going on? Has he crossed me off his list? Then the thought comes: I'll bet he has taken that temporary job at the post office. He had been wanting to make some money. He'll be calling Saturday, when he'll be free. I feel better. I have chosen to trust George. I'll bet he's got a really good reason.

On Friday morning Tom calls and tells me he had been to a rock concert the night before, and there was George about six rows ahead of him. That does it! Or does it? I'll bet relatives came and George had to show them around town. I'll bet he's really bothered by the way his desire to play racquetball with me is being frustrated. I'll bet he's even more frustrated about it than I am.

Is it reasonable for me to keep believing? Am I still able to believe? Is choosing to believe in George's friendship still challenging me?

We choose to believe or we choose not to believe. In the face of growing evidence, do I succumb and decide that he has changed his mind about me? Or do I choose to believe that George will surely come through, and when he does, he'll have a very good explanation for all the evidence of his neglect.

What if I got a letter from George telling me he was fed up with racquetball and with me? This kind of evidence would eliminate faith as a free choice. I could always imagine it was a joke or that he had been drugged by his parents who hate me, but I would be leaving the real world were I to choose that, and my persistence in treating George as a person who wants my friendship would lead to unpleasant encounters.

This is the type of choice Jesus is making: faith choices.

He encounters terrible human suffering. It can mean that God does not care for these people. But it can be that God is filled with compassion for these people. Jesus himself experiences great compassion for them. He chooses to believe that God does also, that God has been there before him, and that, as a matter of fact, his own compassion is nothing but a share in God's. He has inherited his compassion from God.

It isn't obvious to Jesus that God is filled with love for the world. It's a faith choice. He chooses to believe—of the many reasonable options—that God is actually the most loving God of all, the most filled with affection for us that could be imagined.

When we look at the world, it is not obvious that the world's creator is filled with love. Some very reasonable people do not believe it at all. But neither does the evidence we have rule it out. Oh no? What of the suffering? How can I believe in a God who is filled with affection for me when I am suffering and God does nothing? Or, more objectively, how can you expect me to believe that this starving African child has for his God a person filled with affection for him? Jesus asks that same question.

When we see suffering, we ask, Where is God? When Jesus sees human suffering, he asks, Where is God? How can Jesus have ever come to preach to people about such goodness unless he first faced that problem in his own consciousness.

It's as if we are walking with someone, and we pass a most wretched child, crippled, thin, and covered with grime. You say to me, "She is the only child of the wealthiest man in Baltimore." How can you expect me to believe that?

Jesus knows that the higher we place God's goodness, the more difficult it becomes to believe, because we tend to tie it to the evidence. This really isn't believing at all. Believing is free. Does the suffering prove that there is no such goodness?

In the parables of the seed, Jesus demonstrates the radical nature of true faith. It is a conviction about what is not seen. It flows from a free decision to assume that God is to be trusted totally. As the evidence disappears, the decision to believe becomes more and more willful, decisive, involving. It fixes its attention on the spectacular goodness, and reaffirms it, rechooses it in every new situation. Each individual act stems from a fundamental decision that is coming to birth at the deepest personal level.

For Jesus this is a free and most bold insistence on the existence of a God who relates to the world with unimaginable tenderness.

As he moves through his public life and any evidence he has for such goodness becomes less and less obvious, he is, of course, tempted to withdraw himself from that path of trust. To stay on the path is going to involve more and more of his personal energy, his freedom.

89

In the story about George home for the holiday, the evidence for trusting in George's affection diminishes. But the option to believe remains. In some relationships the choice approaches an absolute decision to trust, but it never reaches that level of finality in human life.

With Jesus too there is always a call to choose at ever-deeper levels.

In the face of human suffering he summons up scenarios that would clothe his decision to believe. "How can you believe that this confused and abandoned flock is in God's care?" "Ah, it's like this: God works like a seed in the ground, hidden from view but thoroughly effective!" So he expresses again the spectacular good news of God's kindness despite appearances to the contrary.

Of course beneath the image of God's working as a seed is a choice Jesus is making: I shall not turn away from the God of the prophets. They were not wrong. I shall not live in a world abandoned by its God. I choose to live my life taking for granted that this lost sheep is even now being sought with a divine energy that cannot rest until the sheep is found. But while I can see the lost sheep so clearly, the shepherd hastening to its rescue is invisible.

Is the shepherd there? You have a choice. So does Jesus, and he focuses directly on that choice. His life becomes centered upon it. He himself becomes a certain pattern of choosing, an ever more willful and deliberate and involved use of freedom.

We can easily avoid having to choose. All we need do is avoid the sight of the lost sheep. In this evasion of reality our culture will cooperate mightily. Detours will be constructed for us. Unless we make a deliberate effort to see the lost sheep, we will never be bothered by them. As we go down the path of avoidance, since there will be no lost sheep in our experience of the world (at least, none that hasn't brought this lostness on itself), we will not be forced to choose between an image of an indifferent God (or no God at all) and the hastening shepherd God whom Jesus preaches. We can settle in comfortably with a god who, although he's not so spectacular as all that, is good to have around, who will open the gate when we have completed our journey, a god who keeps us on our toes, who helps those who help themselves.

But Jesus keeps choosing to face those areas where the evidence for God's providence is most meager. His life revolves more and more completely around the question of faith. The lack of decisive evidence allows us to let our fancy roam. All we see is a lost sheep. Whether there is a shepherd and the nature of his activity are up for grabs. I can imagine that there is no shepherd at all and the sheep's bleating is only going to lead all the sooner to his being eaten by a wolf. Or I can imagine some level of indifference: a shepherd, having noticed he's one short, waits for a few more minutes, then he goes in to eat and retire, changing his count to ninety-nine.

As long as this question stays "out there" and theoretical, it is easy to be satisfied with a shepherd constructed in our own image—one who is good to the cooperative but who lets the uncooperative go their way. But once I am involved personally—because either someone I love is now the abandoned sheep or I myself seem abandoned—I can be forced to choose. Then it will happen that I can believe only in a God far better or far worse than the one I have been living with. Jesus seeks situations such as these—where we are forced to choose because we identify with the lost sheep. His affection is so strong that he constantly encounters such situations.

That same faith problem—How can God be good when there is so much suffering?—gradually draws all of Jesus' attention and energy. He makes himself into a response to that one element in our world: human suffering. It is here that the goodness of God is most challenged. It is here that Jesus comes to dwell. His love for his brothers and sisters guarantees that for him the problem of evil is not theoretical or the relatively rare experience. We ourselves can get away from it because the great mass of sufferers are not in our circle of affection. We do not identify with them. But not so with Jesus.

For him it is a central experience. Sometimes after a house fire, a survivor will be faced with the deaths of those close to him and with visiting others with burn wounds. For Jesus they are all his—the lepers, the possessed, the lame, the blind, the hungry, all his own. The problem of evil cannot be escaped. His choosing to love these people forces him to make constant faith choices.

As he watches his mission fail, he is faced again with a choice. Doesn't their refusal signify final disaster for them? Won't God now turn away and acknowledge that Jesus has done all he can but to no avail? The sheep is jumping from the shepherd's arms, kicking vigorously, and is fleeing back into the thicket.

Still Jesus feels for them in their blindness. Surely God does too. God will find a way. God has already, no doubt, found a way and will be leading Jesus into it. Jesus is not forced to believe this by any evidence. This is a faith choice of his. When we say that he knows that God will not abandon Israel, we are talking of a decision he makes: he chooses to believe that. All his knowledge of God's trustworthiness is a faith knowledge, a knowledge based on his free decision to believe.

This free decision of his to believe in a trustworthy God is our salvation.

Prayer Exercise

Here is another exercise that is much more effective if you take it one step at a time. Don't read it beforehand.

Imagine yourself sitting on the street corner of a city you know well. You are sitting there invisible. People are passing. Realistic people though all strangers. Watch them pass.

Notice how they are dressed, their facial expressions, the different sizes and shapes, tall, thin, and so on. Notice the way they walk, where they look.

Focus on one person. Where is he coming from? (Make up a likely answer.) Where is he going? Try another. What is she thinking about? What is she hoping for, planning? Try four or five more.

Close your eyes and just hear the noises on the street. What do you feel about these people, about the whole scene? Anything at all? Attracted? Repelled? Comfortable?

Notice that there has been someone else watching the scene with you. It is the Father. Watch him as people pass. What is his reaction to this scene? To that person? To this person? To what that person is thinking?

Is the Father's reaction like yours? How is it different?

What could God do about this scene that isn't already being done? (Maybe nothing will occur to you.) As a loving father, what "should" God do? What would Zeus or Buddha do? What would you do if you were God? In other words, explore the choices God has.

92

What does God do about it? Notice how the street corner remains the same to all appearances. It is just as it was five, twenty-five, even a thousand years ago. Notice how God appears to do nothing at all.

Enter God's presence and ask: Lord, show me how little I love, and how little I trust you.

Did the images flow easily? What were your reactions to the various people? Did you experience any negative feelings like indifference, or even disgust, contempt, or anger?

On another occasion you may use a different scene: your dinner table, imagining those you live with; your workplace, perhaps some meeting of those you work with. You are always invisible, observing, exploring the difference between you and God, between where you are and where you could be.

Chapter Sixteen

In two other parables of unexpected goodness Jesus introduces the new element, the surprising rejection.

The king invites all to the banquet for his son's wedding. Because the hall is so huge and because the king can't bear the thought of an empty seat, he brings in even those who sleep behind hedges and wander the roads homeless. He dresses them up. They are all there waiting. Now the wedding party begins to arrive preceded by the royal relatives. But when the royal dukes see the great crowds—why, there are people there they don't even know!—they begin to murmur among themselves. Angrily they move toward the exit and out they go.

After all, if everyone is invited, what's the use of going?

That is what is beneath the resistance to Jesus' preaching—self-esteem. These guests get all their meaning from the differences between being royal and not being royal. A consciousness of personal worth that has been built up over the years is proving to be a massive block to hearing the good news. "I have kept all these commandments from my youth." And now I must learn how to be forgiven!

Jesus comments, "Nobody who has been drinking old wine wants new. He says, 'The old is good'" (Luke 5:39 NJB). This new approach is rejected. The more wealthy you are in the old, the less ready you are to change. Revolutions are not welcomed by establishments.

In the second parable the owner of the vineyard has workers who work for different lengths of time. Some begin early and work all day, but a number begin at noon, and a few begin late and work only one hour. The vineyard owner is moved with compassion: each of his workers needs his pay, even though some have not earned it.

94

Jesus imagines this spectacular owner who responds to his workers' needs. It's very uncapitalistic, and such an owner cannot long be in business. But it is Jesus' story and that's how he tells it. He forces it on us: God is relating to the neediness in you! That's the new wine.

Now, as he senses the mortal nature of the resistance to himself, he develops the parable a bit more. In addition to the delight of the latecomers who get paid first—and for a full day's work—murmuring arises from those who have worked all day. They slaved, much like the elder brother. They built up a sense of worth. They cooperated. Now it turns out they should have played football until late in the day, put in an hour's work, and they'd be just as well off. It's not fair.

It's like Zacchaeus. He makes plenty of money by ignoring God's commandments. We keep to the Law and have to sweat to get by. But we do it because we know it is God's will and leads to salvation. A lifetime of this, and teaching our children to respect the Law of God. And now this "prophet" says that salvation is available for Zacchaeus too. It's not fair. In fact it can't be true. The old wine is better. Let us get rid of this new vintage.

They murmur. Jesus puts words into the vineyard owner's mouth. "Have I no right to do what I like with my own?" (Matt. 20:15 NJB). The Kingdom is God's and it is promised not to the worthy but to the children. A sense of deserving it is catastrophic. Then Jesus has the owner ask the question that Jesus himself asked: "Why should you be envious because I am generous?" (Matt. 20:15 NJB).

Like the elder brother, they spend their time in a salary mind-set, and now they are confronted with a change of the rules in the middle of the game. This kind of owner isn't welcome around here.

This kind of God is unacceptable. Jesus puts in God's mouth the words "I choose" (Matt. 20:14 NJB). That's what you are up against. A God who chooses. A God who makes a personal decision.

God will not change. If you insist that the prodigal must be ejected—or at least put in his place—before you enter the banquet, you will never enter, because God will not change this decision. If you want to go away unhappy, the decision is ultimately yours, for God has decided to be generous and God is standing on the right to do as God pleases with what is his. God is not going to be refashioned into your image of God! It would not be God. Only this is God—this spectacular kindness to the unworthy. This is what God has really been like all along. It was hidden from us, but it was known to God all along, and God was eager to reveal it. Now in Jesus this true face of God is at last being revealed.

At the appearance of God's true face, a new level of human malice is revealed also. Jesus' teaching of God's hidden goodness lays bare also a horror, a horror hidden within the human heart, the secret malice concealed within (Luke 2:35).

As the workers who worked all day come to get paid, they are tired but very happy. They will be getting what they need to live for another day. After the payments have been made, though, they are unhappy. Even though they have not had even a small part of their pay taken away, their happiness has been taken away. Their happiness is revealed to be dependent on the fact that there will be some who will not receive enough to feed their families.

This is what Jesus sees in people—a happiness that rests on the misery of others. This is what makes the Kingdom unacceptable, a piece of bad news. Here is the heart of the resistance he is encountering, an imbedded competitiveness.

What if I am one of those who works all day, and one of the lazy fellows who works only an hour is my sister's husband. She has three children and can barely scrape by with that husband of hers. My wife helps out all she can with food and clothes, but there's a limit because we are not wealthy either. Then perhaps when I see him get paid enough to buy a good meal for the family, I might be happy as I picture my sister's joy when she sees the money.

That is love. It is identifying with the one who receives what she needs. It is the same as if you did me a favor. When you feed my sister's children out of your own kindness, you feed me.

When you give a banquet to my long-lost brother, you give a banquet to me. Because I identify myself with him, any favor you do to him, you do to me. Had he loved, the elder brother would have seen the banquet as for himself. "Yes, I know this brother of mine doesn't deserve it, but I do love him and he does need it."

At times we pray that someone we love who has gone into a distant place will be treated kindly in his loneliness by some family there. It's like a mother bringing her child to nursery school. "May he find a friend there, someone who will notice his needs."

But why should I identify with this worthless fellow's needs? Because otherwise you will never become like God, for the heart of God is like this. Fortunately for all worthless fellows.

Once you measure yourself honestly against the love command, you can see within yourself an instinctive revulsion from real love, a self-centeredness that is unforgiveable. Then Jesus' words of forgiveness become your very life.

In respect to God and God's promises and the Kingdom, none of us has worked all day. It can come to each only as a free gift. So in each of the parables Jesus has someone who is very conscious of his personal worth and very conscious of the differences between people. Jesus raises for them the love command. In parable after parable the true nature of love is distinguished from its artificial forms. Love is of the heart and the affections. Love identifies me with the other.

When someone I love is in need, I notice it. I have special eyes for that. I respond without any thought of recompense. I am eager to be able to help, and I count what I do as little compared to what I would like to do. I hear the needs of the other and take action with energy and speed.

The world of salary is different. In that earning world I count up what I have done and expect recompense. The self measures its giving with great care and conscious attention. It fears the entry of goodness and kindness and need into its calculations. Because of this fear it needs to be forgiven.

You see the judge surrounded by pots and jars and cups and cans and even a barrel and a few large containers, and behind him you can see four or five immense cartons—one is as big as a boxcar. Hovering over them is a jar the size of a mountain.

The judge says, "All of these containers, even the largest, is filled with kindness and forgiveness. You must pick out the container that you want me to use on you on the Day of Judgment."

"Do you mean I get to pick that?! There must be a catch. If I can pick the container, I will live my life at peace,

97

never worried about the final judgment. It can't be. There's a catch?"

"Yes, there is. During your life you must use that same container in your dealings with others."

"Because the measure you use will be the measure used for you" (Luke 6:38).

Jesus raises the love command. When he is asked for the central command, he brings up love. He puts so much emphasis upon it that to us it appears exaggerated.

> Everyone who is angry with his brother shall be liable to judgment; whoever insults his brother shall be liable to the council, and whoever says, "You fool!" shall be liable to the hell of fire. (Matt. 5:22 RSV)

As John McKenzie puts it in his commentary on this passage, "Interpreters are deceived by the severity of Jesus, and they cannot believe that He speaks so sternly of simple, abusive language."*

The Jesus who speaks like this is very much a man who wants to wake people up to a mortal and hidden danger present in their lives. Because you are not a murderer you tend to feel yourself a law-abiding person. Yet the rejection of Jesus' preaching is coming from people who are not murderers. Some other evil—hidden from the eye, for they appear to be devout—is present and is leading them to the destructive choice of rejecting Jesus.

He carefully locates the infection within them. He describes it for them and he spells out the fact: Danger. Mortal Danger. Anger and contempt are toxic. They contradict the good news. They shrink from it. The love command is given to you not as a burden you must carry but as a form of preaching the good news. An event has actually occurred that so radically affects the heart of all reality that "turning the other cheek" and "forgiving your enemies" is now appropriate, reasonable behavior.

Why does he use that word *enemy*? How different his challenge

* "The Gospel According to Matthew," in R. E. Brown, J. A. Fitzmyer, R. E. Murphy, eds., *The Jerome Biblical Commentary* (Englewood Cliffs, NJ: Prentice-Hall, 1968), 2:71.

would be had he not used it. But he does use it, and it is most revealing of his mind. If we could make Jesus over into one we would like, this word would drop out. In practice it very often does become neutralized, irrelevant. "I have no real enemies. Jesus is not speaking to my problems." But, of course, he meant by "enemy" one who is unfair to us, who speaks unfairly about us, or treats us unfairly, or even merely thinks unfairly of us. If I can find none of these in my life, I should ask some friend to help me. Friends can usually provide a short list of those we resent. To us the resentment appears harmless and trivial—and quite justifiable. To Jesus it is a mortal infection and, if not taken care of, will surely lead to a refusal to enter the wedding banquet. We cannot see how it's all that important, like an alcoholic arguing that one drink never hurt. Jesus is like a friend, using every means at his disposal to wake us up to the peril contained in our competitiveness, our indifference, our toleration for judgment and resentment.

We find his language excessive. The evils he singles out are just not that bad. We think he's like a worried mother warning her son of pneumonia if he fails to wear his galoshes.

But Jesus is most clear. That very harmless little fault, as you call it, will keep you from the Kingdom. That limited love that satisfies your conscience does not satisfy the command. It is not love at all.

> A man lives on a farm with ten members of his family. He gets along well with and really loves eight of them. There are just two whom he feels he does not love. He feels he is doing well.
>
> When he comes to the judge, the judge says, "Do the eight love you back?"
>
> "Of course. It's been wonderful," says the man.
>
> Then the judge says, "Let's not count those eight, then, in evaluating you. Because when you love those who love you, there's nothing there. Even the tax-collectors do that! Even the pagans do that! That doesn't really count." (Matt. 5:46–47)

"You must therefore set no bounds to your love, just as your heavenly Father sets none to his" (Matt. 5:48). "Love your enemies and do good to them, and lend without any hope of return. You will have a great reward, and you will be children of the Most High, for he himself is kind to the ungrateful and the wicked" (Luke 6:34–35).

Here is the kernel: The good news is precisely that God is like that, and there is no becoming a child of God unless I become like him.

"Why do you call me, 'Lord, Lord,' and not do what I say?" (Luke 6:46 NJB). This is the cry of a man whose words are being watered down and interpreted away.

Even among his disciples the infection is present. There is a competitiveness that they know he does not like so they try to indulge in it only when he is not around. His warnings are not taken to heart.

It is such a subtle thing. The beginnings appear so harmless, so unimportant. They don't seem to be the beginning of anything. It's like a small cut. Jesus compares it to a yeast just as he compares God's way of working to a yeast. It is so insignificant that it can easily be missed. But it is deadly.

> Keep your eyes open,
> and be on your guard against the yeast
> of the Pharisees and Sadducees. (Matt. 16:6 NJB)

This evil requires alertness, open-eyed attention. It enters easily without our notice. To be free requires being on guard, on the lookout for it all the time. It is constantly seeking to enter.

The pious hypocrite is the final phase of the infection. He is locked into a system of evaluating people's lives.

It has two parts. In order to feel good about myself, in order to have that self-esteem we feel is so necessary, I remember every little score in my favor, and I excuse and forget my failings. I build an image of myself as a cooperative fellow.

I notice and remember the faults of others. I can offer to help my brother's slightest fault: "Let me take that splinter out of your eye." "Look, there is a great log in your own. Hypocrite" (Matt. 7:4–5).

It is a sense of self-esteem based on competitiveness. It appears so harmless and it is so deadly. Jesus sees its deadly nature and how it is leading people to reject his preaching.

Prayer Exercise

Do this a step at a time. Go slowly enough to hear Jesus' voice, not just the words he says.

Most are taking a siesta. But a small group is chatting quietly with Jesus—you, Martha, and three of the men. The talk is about the Pharisees and their hostility, and about Herod. Peter and Martha do most of the talking. There is a pause, and Jesus says, "Your real enemies are those within your own circle."

You decide to shift the conversation, so you praise Peter for a talk he has given often when on mission, a talk on loving God wholeheartedly. But Jesus returns to his point:

If you don't love the brother who is right there in front of you, how can you say you love God who is invisible?

Judas says, "I think Peter is as good a preacher as I've ever heard." Peter is delighted but embarrassed. John adds, "I heard that talk he gives on loving God and it really touched the crowd." Jesus says, "If anyone says, 'I love God,' but keeps on hating his brother, he's a liar."

This stops the chatter. Jesus is insisting:

I demand that you love each other
even as I love you.
Then your cup of joy will overflow.

He looks down and everyone is still. "You are not my slaves: you are my friends. If you obey me."

Then he says again, "I demand that you love each other."

John says, "But isn't preaching important too?" Jesus replies:

If you had the power to preach
like an angel of heaven,
but you didn't love others,
you would only be making noise.

Ask the Father that Jesus become a more realistic presence in your consciousness.

We become ourselves in our choices. To know me is to know how I choose, what I prefer. Jesus' most personal, most revealing choice was to forgive those who dealt unjustly with him. To know Jesus is to know forgiving love. It is not hard to make the mistake of thinking, "Yes, I want to know Jesus," and never relating it to my preference not to forgive or at least to be free of situations where my forgiving would be called for.

At other times imagine Jesus speaking to the disciples the words of 1 Cor. 13:1–17. Or hear him say the words of 1 John

1:5–6
2:4–11
3:15
4:7–8, 10–12

Chapter Seventeen

Jesus begins to use the same parables in which he had revealed God's Kingdom to explain the opposition that is arising against him. He brings into the parables people who are intensely competitive and who become filled with resentment when they hear the good news.

But a new mood takes over in his preaching also. Here is an example to help get some sense of the very strange impact this later preaching had.

> You like to sit in your front room and watch the street, even though practically nothing ever happens. But you like to wait for the postman that way.
>
> You notice that old Smith has opened his front door twice now and looked at his watch. The postman is late.
>
> But now you see the postman turn the corner. As he reaches the Smiths and starts up toward their porch, the front door comes open and out comes old Smith. He does look somewhat angry.
>
> He has a gun in his hands. The postman raises his hands but Smith's shot hits him in the stomach. Smith bends over the crumpled postman. He's still conscious, begging for mercy, but Smith starts striking him in the head with the revolver until he stops moving.

This is a story of unexpected malice. It is so unpleasant. Yet this is what Jesus puts his hearers through in this new phase of his preaching.

> Listen to another parable.
>
> There was a landowner who planted a vineyard. He fences it round, digs a wine press in it, and builds a tower. Then he leases it to his tenants and goes abroad.

So far it is a humdrum tale. Imagine what it is like to be hearing this from Jesus' lips. Imagine what Jesus feels as he tells it.

When vintage time drew near he sent his servants to the tenants to collect his produce. But the tenants seized his servants, thrashed one, killed another, and stoned a third.

This is not a very likely scenario. But it could happen. Why is he telling us this?

Next he sends some more servants, this time a larger number. They deal with them in the same way.

It is rather violent, but still it involves people who are somewhat hazy and not vividly portrayed. But Jesus has a point to make, and he deliberately steps up the vividness.

> Finally he sends his son to them, thinking,
> "They will respect my son."
> But when the tenants see the son,
> they say to each other,
> "This is the heir. Come on, let us kill him
> and take over his inheritance."

Jesus now actually spells out the acts of violence, the murder. He goes into detail.

> So they seized him
> and threw him out of the vineyard
> and killed him.

Then Jesus invites his hearers to imagine the enormous consequences of such an act. He could have stopped with the son's death, but he has more.

> "Now when the owner of the vineyard comes,
> what will he do to those tenants?"
> They answered,
> "He will bring those wretches
> to a wretched end." (Matt. 21:33–41 NJB)

Jesus introduces into his parables a violence that is at least unexpected and even unrealistic. He wants to describe what is happening around him. A violence is being uncovered by his preaching, a maliciousness that was hidden. Now it is appearing, called forth from its hiding place at the words of Jesus.

Where has it been hiding all along? In the human heart. The human heart is a master at concealing, with an endless energy for hypocrisy that is now yielding up its secrets.

Very early in Jesus' public career, John the evangelist tells us, although many believed in him,

> Jesus would not trust himself to them
> because he knew them all.
> He needed no one to give him testimony
> about human nature.
> He was well aware of what was in the human heart.
> (John 2:24–25 NAB)

What is it in the human heart that keeps Jesus from trusting people? On another occasion, in the midst of an argument, Jesus spells it out.

> It is from within,
> from the heart,
> that evil intentions emerge:
> fornication, theft, murder, adultery, avarice,
> malice, deceit, indecency, envy, slander, pride, folly.
> All these evil things come from within. (Mark 7:21–22 NJB)

This is not our familiar Jesus. It is an area of his personality we do not linger on. He sees in the human heart an animosity toward others that alienates us from God and causes our lives to brim with anxiety. Humans behave like possessed people.

To cure the heart, the infection long hidden must first be exposed. The competitiveness that darkens even family life must be brought out and seen. "Do not suppose that I have come to bring peace to the earth: it is not peace I have come to bring, but a sword" (Matt. 10:34 NJB).

Who is this Jesus? What is moving him to speak so? There is no salvation apart from truth. There is no magic cure: "Doctor, do whatever you want, just don't tell me!" No, the truth that is hidden will be exposed. "For I have come to set son against father, daughter against mother. . . . A person's enemies will be the members of his own household" (Matt. 10:35–36 NJB).

Jesus is experiencing this truth. His own are rejecting him. Already, before he began to preach, this rejection was within them, in their heart. They only appeared to be eager for the truth. In their depths a yeast had been at work, an infection had been spreading secretly. All that was needed to bring it out was the light held up to it by Jesus' preaching.

It is hard to avoid his words. They stab to the heart and expose the self as so different from what appears. That light has to be put out.

It is from Micah that Jesus draws this text. It struck him as true, as the very words to express what he is now experiencing.

> How wretched I am,
> a harvester in summertime,
> like a gleaner at the vintage:
> not a single cluster to eat,
> none of those early figs I love! (Mic. 7:1 NJB)

He believes in a great harvest, and he is now finding nothing at all to reap.

> The faithful have vanished from the land:
> there is no one honest left.
> All of them are on the alert for blood,
> every man hunting his brother with a net.
> (Mic. 7:2 NJB)

Exactly. It is the vision of the human heart. "The best of them is like a briar, the most honest of them like a thorn-hedge" (Mic. 7:4 NJB). It is like a psalm, a prayer. It is in Jesus' memory from his student days, when he had memorized it. Now it comes up into his consciousness. It becomes his prayer.

> Now from the north their punishment approaches!
> That will be when they are confounded!
> Trust no neighbor,
> put no confidence in a friend;
> do not open your mouth
> to the wife who shares your bed.
> For son insults father,
> daughter rebels against mother,
> daughter-in-law against mother-in-law;

106

a person's enemies come from within
the household itself. (Mic. 7:4–6 NJB)

It had all been seen before. He is not alone in his vision. It is
hard to believe that to everyone else things are so normal. He sees
the heart and the violence. When he first speaks of it to Peter, Peter
rejects it and tries to persuade him otherwise. To Peter it looks
small, not worth the terrible, heavy language.

But Jesus sees it. And someone has seen it before him. It is not
beyond God's care.

But I shall look to the LORD,
my hope is in the God who will save me;
my God will hear me. (Mic. 7:7 NJB)

Now Jesus changes the parable of the wedding banquet.

Once again the banquet is ready and the invitations go out. But
the invited do not come. An unexpected refusal. But the king
persists:

Next he sends some more servants with the
words, "Tell those who have been invited:
Look, my banquet is all prepared, my oxen and
fattened cattle have been slaughtered,
everything is ready. Come to the wedding."
(Matt. 22:4 NJB)

It has all the freshness of those early days when the great
crowds marveled at the power of his speech. But now he introduces
the bizarre.

But they are not interested:
one goes off to his farm,
another to his business,
and the rest seize his servants,
maltreat them and kill them. (Matt. 22:5–6 NJB)

Suddenly old Smith shoots down the postman. To refuse an
invitation to a banquet—that happens. But do we kill the messengers? Isn't this a most unrealistic twist? This is the way Jesus
sees it, a most unprovoked malice. An intent so malicious it is hard
to believe, and yet that is precisely what he is faced with.

107

Now he changes the image of the king. He pours a violence into him also.

> The king is furious.
> He despatches his troops,
> destroys those murderers,
> and burns their town. (Matt. 22:7 NJB)

The air is filled with threats of violence. What is coming up from the depths of the human heart will lead to the destruction of the human heart itself.

Into Jesus' preaching comes a burning of towns. Jesus makes a strange addition to the parable of the talents also. The master is seeking to be made king; he entrusts the talents to his servants and goes off to Rome seeking the emperor's nod. But while he is there, some people from his country arrive and urge the emperor not to choose him as king. "We do not want this man to be our king" (Luke 19:14 NJB).

Does Jesus recall this image from Psalm 2? "Princes plot together against the LORD and his anointed" (Ps. 2:2 NJB). It enables Jesus to conclude the parable with an image of unmitigated violence. The master is chosen king and returns, rewarding the faithful servants and punishing the wicked one who had let the talent stay idle. Now he turns to his aides and orders:

> As for my enemies
> who do not want me for their king,
> bring them here
> and execute them in my presence. (Luke 19:27 NJB)

Jesus is reading the hearts of his enemies as well. Beneath their law-abiding surface is a violent lawlessness. He uses these images of violence both to describe the real nature of the heart and the terrifying destruction that looms ahead for them.

But he sees the enemy at work among his own also. A competitiveness that is carefully hidden is at work there too. In this next example we can glimpse Jesus' way of dealing with it.

At times we are so unfairly treated by someone that we finally write them off. "Fool me twice, shame on me." At times, though, it's not just twice but a long pattern of being betrayed by this person that ends in a decision to ignore them, to be unresponsive, to live my life apart from them, to act as if nothing they say is of any importance.

"How do you feel toward her?" "Totally indifferent. Nothing she says interests me." Indifference seems a morally neutral state. It's not exactly love but neither is it hate. It's in between and that's neutral. It's the way we react to people we don't know. It's not condemned in the gospel.

We don't mind seeing ourselves in this attitude. It's an acceptable self-image even apart from our ample justification for it.

Contempt, though, is an emotion we do not enjoy seeing in ourselves. It is strongly and vehemently condemned in the gospel. Anger too. It is painful to see myself filled with anger.

But very often indifference is just the name we give to what in the heart is actually contempt, a most condemnable attitude. We may have a powerful contempt and not know it. If we are asked whether we hold anyone in contempt, we deny it and feel sincere in our denial. The contempt is buried. It is known now only to others, especially, of course, to the person we contemn. It is so difficult to deal with someone who has contempt for you and is quite unaware of it!

What can Jesus do to awaken people to the absence of love in their heart? Here is one of his efforts.

He imagines a meeting between a man who is in debt and the man who lends him the money. The debt is overdue, long overdue, and the man who owes the money has been on the run, carefully keeping out of the way. You may have met people like that: they borrow and become scarce. Sometimes they make the newspapers, because they've been doing it for years, and finally they get caught.

In this case the borrower is unlucky and runs into him. The man who owes the debt begins his usual line, "I'll pay you first of the month, never fear. Here's where you can reach me." But the other man ignores him and summons the police.

Some people who are watching know both men well. When they see what was happening, they are "deeply disturbed" (Matt. 18:31). Matthew uses this same phrase to describe the apostles' reaction to Jesus' words predicting his passion (Matt. 17:23).

Why are the people so upset? They are disturbed at the action of the man who lent the money. His decision not to let the other man go thoroughly shakes the bystanders. They are all amazed at his refusal to let the other man off.

Yet the man's behavior seems quite correct. How can such behavior be seen as criminal? To see the truth beneath this apparently correct behavior you need to know a bit of this man's story. He himself—as the bystanders well know—has just that morning wept and told of a terrible ruin hanging over him: he was himself in debt too far and was on his way to trial. His life was finished and his family impoverished. People had sympathized with him as he walked to the courthouse. They had rejoiced with him when he returned a free man. He had been let off, the whole debt canceled.

This explains how an apparently justifiable act becomes repulsive. By being forgiven, he has lost any claim to justice. His whole life rests on being forgiven. It has a totally new base. Yet he goes back to his old way and demands that justice be done.

The image has a certain implausibility to it. How can anyone who has just been treated so mercifully not, in his joy, be forgiving? Even Jesus gives us the parable about how love flows into the heart of one who has been forgiven much. It works automatically. You are about to be condemned, and suddenly, from a quite unexpected corner, deliverance! Joy floods the heart and expresses itself in actions. Like Magdalene and Zacchaeus.

Still, Jesus sees in people a remarkable persistence in demanding justice, no matter how much they talk of their need for God's mercy. A human capacity for forgetting God's kindness enables us to see ourselves deserving justice. We are willing to go through motions and all the while refuse to forgive from the heart.

In that refusal to forgive from the heart, the parable reveals within me a denial that I myself stand only within God's mercy. I deny the whole process of being saved. We behave this way because we forget how we are dealt with. When we refuse to forgive from the heart, we deny the good news.

Jesus describes violence on the part of the owner of the vineyard, the king who gives the banquet, and the master who seeks to be made king. It suggests a violence present in God toward those who refuse to love. In this parable Jesus draws the parallel explicitly and composes an image of his heavenly Father inflicting great pain.

And in his anger, the master handed him over
to the torturers
till he should pay all his debt.
And that is how
my heavenly Father will deal with you
unless you each forgive your brother
from your heart. (Matt. 18:34–35 NJB)

What a frightening image — or at least an image intended by its inventor to frighten. The heavenly Father handing me over to torturers!

Prayer Exercise

Jesus preached good news: God is a God of unexpected goodness. But, unlike Jonah, Jesus met with fierce opposition.

He turned to parables to express his experience. He made up a parable that portrayed God with an enemy: his Father with an enemy (Matt. 13:24–30).

Does this parable help you to explain the world? Does your God have an enemy?

Jesus created parables that located the core of this opposition to him in the unloving heart. What keeps us from accepting the good news? What keeps us from deep faith? What keeps us from accepting an invitation to a banquet? Jealousy, envy, judgment, resentment, contempt, unlove.

Do you see it this way? Is there any real connection between your relations with some very unpleasant and unfair people and your faith in God?

Jesus told parables to explain why he was not welcomed, parables of unexpected malice.

Matt. 20:10–16
Matt. 18:23–35
Matt. 21:33–41
Matt. 22:1–10
Luke 14:16–24

Luke 15:25–32
Luke 19:14–27

What is the look on his face as Jesus faces his listeners with these parables? Imagine his face, his eyes. What is he hoping will happen as a result of his words? What is the most he can hope for, his wildest dreams?

What are his feelings as he creates these parables?

Can you imagine him intending this message for you? Looking your way as he speaks a crucial sentence?

Chapter Eighteen

To the very end of Jesus' public life, his contemporaries link the role of John the Baptist with Jesus. But remember how carefully Jesus distinguishes between his own image of the messiah and the image the Baptist preached.

On one occasion Jesus puts this difference into an image. He sees children playing in the marketplace. Some have collected sticks and a broken pot or two and have made themselves into a band. They pretend to play on pipes, and they pipe out a dance, but the other children just sit there and watch. Nobody dances. So the band switches to a funeral march. But nobody joins the procession.

This is the story of John and Jesus.

"For John came neither eating nor drinking . . ." Jesus had noticed that in John.

> And they say, "He is possessed."
> The Son of Man came, eating and drinking,
> and they say,
> "Look, a glutton and a drunkard,
> a friend of tax-collectors and sinners."
> (Matt. 11:18–19 NJB)

John was so austere, so strict, and his preaching was filled with the threat of violence. People said he was diabolical. But Jesus is so different that people must find a new angle to write him off—he is not like a prophet at all! He is soft, indulgent, and easy on sinners. Where is the prophetic fire?

That was at the beginning of his public life, but now it is changing. In the light of the rejection of the messiah, Jesus' own parables are becoming violent. Jesus sees a great need to wake people up. A terrible danger is moving toward them. A catastrophe is in their direct path. Unless they choose to change, they will be destroyed. A violence like John's enters into Jesus' preaching.

With this new tone in his preaching, Jesus himself is called mad and possessed, diabolical.

All of God's newly revealed kindness does not change the fact that we are free. Our choices are decisive and weighted with eternal consequences.

Yet it doesn't appear so. Life seems so much less dramatic than all that. The differences between people seem so small that it's hard to believe that my one neighbor will suffer endless pain while my other neighbor will spend an eternity in the joyful embrace of God. Yet this is Jesus' clear conviction. This conviction sets him on his path now, a path of warning: Danger!

When you choose to refuse to forgive, you kill your God. Your life is not a minor part on the stage of reality but a starring role. By God's decision you are invited into God's own friendship. At the end of your life, you will be the one who accepts this offer and is God's intimate friend, or you will refuse that offer and become a blazing anger and an unquenchable frustration. There are no other options.

God's kindness makes our lives dangerous. With the Son's coming we become players in a drama where we can kill him. Sinners are more aware of the possibilities of malice in their lives, but the devout easily miss it. The devout are tempted to see themselves as incapable of putting God to death. Because they refuse to imagine it as a realistic possibility, they run the risk of its happening. Any time we refuse to face a likely outcome, we become incapable of taking steps to avoid it.

By his coming Jesus brings a new danger. The coming of the messiah in this generation places this generation in danger of killing the messiah. No one had ever imagined it possible. Jesus now fills his preaching with warnings. He must wake people up from their comfortable slumber. He must warn them of the poison they take in when they reject the path of forgiving and caring, when they insist on distinguishing between the worthy and the unworthy. It is a distinction based on hypocrisy, and it includes a refusal of the good news: that God loves the unworthy. The consequences of dishonesty are eternal suffering.

At the end there will be no one in the middle. Everyone will have become either a yes or a no, even though as we look at their lives they seem so alike. Jesus imagines the moment when the hearts of all will be laid bare:

> I tell you, on that night,
> when two are in one bed,
> one will be taken, the other left;
> when two women are grinding corn together,
> one will be taken, the other left. (Luke 17:34–35 NJB)

He sees beneath the appearances. We all seem so similar— almost like the bell curve for grading tests. Some few appear rather savage, and some others border on that. A few seem saintly. But most appear ordinary. He warns that it is not so in reality. In each one's life there is coming to birth a simple yes or a totally solidified no. There is no in-between.

But human life is so regular and ordinary and commonplace. It's so unlikely that anything of cosmic importance is taking place. It's all so undramatic that prophets seem a bit deranged.

This family has a nice dinner. There's a good wine, and the spirit is friendly. Next door, the oldest girl is going to be married, so the parents are talking about the dowry, and the girl herself is nervous about leaving her home. Across the street in the very large house, plans are afoot to purchase a new vacation home. Everybody in the family is getting in on it. The excitement is high. What a difference it will make in the years to come.

Jesus imagines how ordinary life seems:

> People were eating and drinking,
> buying and selling,
> planting and building,
> but the day Lot left Sodom,
> it rained fire and brimstone from heaven
> and it destroyed them all. (Luke 17:28–29 NJB)

How does one persuade people that the ordinary flow of human life from day to day is no guarantee that all is well? He brilliantly re-creates in his imagination what it was like the day before the Flood. How everyday they were.

For in those days before the Flood
people were eating, drinking,
taking wives, taking husbands,
right up to the day Noah went into the ark,
and they suspected nothing
till the Flood came and swept them all away.
(Matt. 24:37–39 NJB)

The commonplace appearance of human life is no guarantee. Catastrophe is in the wings ready to come on stage. The sense that your life is humdrum will not protect you from being involved in killing God. Your small decision to forgive or not to forgive will lead to your becoming a child of God or to your expulsion from his presence into never-ending pain. Your unimportant and unremembered decision to give a cup of water or to refuse one will result in a curse from the lips of Jesus or lead to the glory of being welcomed by him into paradise. "As it was in Noah's day so will it be when the Son of Man comes" (Matt. 24:37 NJB).

He will separate people one from another, the prodigal from his elder brother, Dives from Lazarus. He will act as a shepherd does when he divides the sheep from the goats. There will be only the two classes of people.

Go away from me,
with your curse upon you,
to the eternal fire
prepared for the devil and his angels. (Matt. 25:41 NJB)

Nowadays we hear the assurance that no one is in hell. Such an assurance plays no part in Jesus' convictions. He goes to great lengths to warn of it, and he is very aware of how easily we rule it out as a real possibility. We are tempted to make Jesus over into an image more to our own purposes.

On an earlier occasion Jesus had imagined the Judgment Day.

When the Day comes
many will say to me,
"Lord, Lord,
did we not prophesy in your name,
drive out demons in your name,
work many miracles in your name?"

116

Then I shall tell them to their faces:
  I have never known you;
   away from me all evil-doers! (Matt. 7:22–23 NJB)

He sits down and eats with sinners. He is moved with compassion at their plight. But there is a time limit. Death. We are so created that we move through our life from day to day—growing and growing—until at last we reach a final use of our freedom, a choice that identifies us permanently, a choice we will never change. This choice is the flower of the seeds we have sown from day to day. She who sows forgiveness and caring—even though she may have considered them unimportant and has forgotten them—now she will be an intimate of God. He who has guarded what was his, and has built his sense of self-esteem by carefully noticing his scores, he will be reminded of the world of need that he has ignored. He will be driven off.

Prayer Exercise

Take this one paragraph at a time.

It is the siesta hour, but you are not sleepy. You are in Thomas's house in Bethsaida, right on the town square. You walk out on the covered balcony. You sit and look down on the people in the square. Even though it is siesta time, there are quite a few people.

Notice how they are dressed, their facial expressions, the different sizes and shapes, how some are tall, some thin, and so on. Notice the way each one walks. How their eyes look about. Notice one person: Where is he coming from? Where is he going? Try another: What is she thinking about, hoping for, planning for? Try four or five more. Notice your feelings about the people.

Suddenly you notice for the first time, on a nearby porch, a cowled figure. It is Jesus. He is gazing at the people, as you are. He looks sad. Follow his eyes as he looks at one of the crowd. What is he thinking? What does he feel as he looks at this person? At that one? Take this slowly.

117

Jesus notices you and waves to you. He comes to Thomas's house and comes out to join you on the balcony.

He says, "I have preached so many times to this town. What do you think will be the outcome of all that work, of all the miracles?" You answer, and there is a conversation. Imagine it.

He then recites from memory Jon. 3:4–10. See if you can hear his voice. Slowly. Then he says to you, "If the miracles I have done here in this town and among these people had been done among pagan peoples, they would have repented long ago, sitting in sackcloth and ashes. It will be easier for the pagans at the Judgment! Alas for Bethsaida!"

You both sit there in silence looking at the people.

Jesus gets up and leaves. You continue to watch. Look at one person carefully. Recall the Jonah passage. Recall Jesus' comment:

> Alas for you, Bethsaida!
> For if the miracles done in you
> had been done in Tyre and Sidon,
> they would have repented long ago,
> sitting in sackcloth and ashes.
> And still, it will not go as hard with Tyre and Sidon
> at the Judgment
> as with you. (Luke 10:13–14 JB)

Enter the presence of God, and ask to know Jesus as he really was and is, a realist, a prophet, a person aware that his mission is of central importance to the life of every human being.

Luke 10:15 can be used in a similar way, with Jesus reciting the words of Isa. 14:13–15 to warn the people of Capernaum.

Chapter Nineteen

No one is unfamiliar with the violent language Jesus uses against the religious leaders of his day: "Do not imitate the hypocrites" (Matt. 6:5 NJB). He calls them blind guides, fit for hell, whitewashed tombs because they look so devout on the surface but are dead within. He calls them serpents, a brood of vipers.

In the beginning the apostles take for granted that the "devout" men will welcome the messiah. Jesus himself had also expected this during that early period when he felt optimistic about his mission.

After one of his clashes with them, when he has called them hypocrites, the disciples come to him and say, "Do you know that the Pharisees were shocked when they heard what you said?" (Matt. 15:12 NJB). As if Jesus had spoken too strongly without realizing. They feel there must be a misunderstanding that should be cleared up.

We are so aware of the radical nature of this clash with these pious hypocrites that we find it hard to imagine that anyone ever expected it to be otherwise.

Remember Jesus' condemnation: "Anyone who calls a brother 'Fool' will answer for it before the Sanhedrin" (Matt. 5:22 NJB). Toward the end of his life he uses the very same words on them. He calls them fools, "Fools and blind!" (Matt. 23:17 NJB). We are accustomed to the image of Jesus attacking hypocrisy and don't find it very threatening. We identify with his hatred of hypocrisy, and we do not see in ourselves any parallel with false piety. We can't imagine ourselves as the hypocrites Jesus condemns. We are more like the ordinary folk that he preached to, a member of the great crowds who loved to listen to him, people like the inhabitants of Capernaum, where he did so much of his work. Or Bethsaida.

Alas for you, Bethsaida!
... It will be more bearable for Tyre and Sidon
at the Judgment than for you.
And as for you, Capernaum,
did you want to be raised high as heaven?
You shall be flung down to hell. (Luke 10:13–15 NJB)

He reaches into his memory to find a text to help these people
see what danger they are in, and he finds a text in Isaiah. The
prophet makes up a song for people to sing when the king of Baby-
lon arrives in hell after his fall from power. Other dead kings mock
him, "How did you come to be thrown to the ground, conqueror
of nations?"

You who used to think to yourself:
I shall scale to the heavens;
higher than the stars of God
I shall set my throne. (Isa. 14:12–13 NJB)

In it Jesus sees a parallel with Capernaum. What a strange passage for Jesus to recall at this moment. His experience at Capernaum has gone terribly sour.

So it's not just the hypocrite leaders. It's the whole chosen people. This hypocrisy is brought home to him with great sharpness
in his rare encounters with pagans. Among them he finds the faith
he seeks in vain among his own people. It astonishes him:

In truth I tell you,
in no one in Israel
have I found faith as great as this. (Matt. 8:10 NJB)

He foresees what it means. The messiah will be welcomed and
effective, but only among the pagans. Who could have foreseen
such a turnabout!

And I tell you
that many will come from east and west
and sit down with Abraham and Isaac and Jacob
at the feast in the Kingdom of Heaven;
but the children of the Kingdom will be thrown out
into the darkness outside,

where there will be weeping and grinding of teeth.
(Matt. 8:11–12 NJB)

He is very frustrated. It could have so easily been different. And it should have been different. Now as he goes through the country, it is with a changed mood.

Through towns and villages he went teaching,
making his way to Jerusalem.
Someone said to him,
"Sir, will there be only a few saved?"
(Luke 13:22–23 NJB)

What a vivid moment. What a good question.

He said to them,
"Try your hardest to enter by the narrow door,
because, I tell you,
many will try to enter and will not succeed."
(Luke 13:23–24 NJB)

Then he produces a picture for them of what the day of salvation will be like.

Once the master of the house has got up
and locked the door,
you may find yourself standing outside
knocking on the door, saying,
"Lord, open to us,"
but he will answer,
"I do not know where you come from." (Luke 13:25 NJB)

He imagines the words he will hear that day as they explain why they should be allowed in, how they broke bread with him and listened as he preached in their own neighborhood. "We once ate and drank in your company; you taught in our streets" (Luke 13:27 NJB).

Here is Jesus projecting himself into their hearts and uncovering for them the basis of their confidence. He must warn them: It will be of no use whatsoever. In fact it will be to their greater shame. Other generations will point the finger at them for their folly in rejecting what had been so long the center of desire for the chosen people.

But he will reply,
"I do not know where you come from;
away from me, all evil-doers!" (Luke 13:27 NJB)

He must make that moment vivid for them, so he lets them hear from his own mouth the words he knows they will hear the Day of Judgment. He calls the words up from his memory. It is Psalm 6.

I am worn out with groaning,
every night I drench my pillow
and soak my bed with tears.
My eyes waste away with vexation,
arrogance from all my foes!
Away from me, all evil-doers! (Ps. 6:6–8 NJB)

Again he pictures the great feast with the surprising outcome.

Then there will be weeping and grinding of teeth,
when you see Abraham and Isaac and Jacob
and all the prophets
in the Kingdom of God,
and you yourselves thrown out,
and people from east and west, from north and south,
will come and sit down at the feast
in the Kingdom of God. (Luke 13:28–29 NJB)

What is he feeling as he steels himself to deliver this warning? The invitation to the banquet of God's spectacular kindness demands honesty and faith.

The crowds got even bigger
and he addressed them:
"This is an evil generation;
it is asking for a sign." (Luke 11:29 NJB)

What frustration! The pagans believed Jonah and yet he worked no sign for them.

Jerusalem, Jerusalem,
you that kill the prophets
and stone those who are sent to you! (Matt. 23:37 NJB)

In his parables he pictures the relationship between God and Israel. God's invitation and the messengers' being killed. Here he speaks it without metaphor. He describes a feeling, a longing that often comes over him.

> How often have I longed
> to gather your children together,
> as a hen gathers her chicks under her wings,
> and you refused. (Matt. 23:37 NJB)

That was his dream. With the Baptist's death, Jesus was forced to rethink his mission. He draws apart from the crowds.

> They made their way through Galilee;
> and he did not want anyone to know,
> because he was instructing his disciples.
> (Mark 9:30–31 NJB)

He himself was being instructed by God in faith.

Prayer Exercise

Do this slowly, one step at a time.

Jesus and the disciples and a huge crowd are on the Mount of the Beatitudes. There is a pause in the preaching. Everyone is eating. You are apart and you are looking out at the crowd, these very ordinary people.

Notice how they are dressed, their facial expressions, the different sizes. Notice how they eat and where they are looking. Pick out one person. What brings her here? Imagine her relationship with the girl at her side. Is it a happy one? Try another. Where will he be eating this evening? What are his hopes for tomorrow? Try four or five others. Notice your own feelings about each one.

You notice that Jesus too is sitting alone, looking out over the crowd.

Someone has caught his attention. Follow his eyes as he watches. He is sad. What is he thinking? What does he feel as he looks at this particular person? At that one? Take this slowly.

Jesus sees you watching him. He beckons you to come and join him. He asks your opinion of the people. You chat for a while.

He then recites Isa. 29:13 NJB.

> Because this people approach me only in words,
> honors me only with lip-service,
> while its heart is far from me . . .

And then Ps. 78:36 JB.

> But though they outwardly flattered [God]
> and used their tongues to lie to him,
> in their hearts they were not true to him,
> they were unfaithful to his covenant.

He then says to you, "This is a faithless and perverse generation. How much longer must I put up with them? It is a wicked generation. On Judgment Day the Queen of the South will rise again, along with this people, and she will condemn them."

> On Judgment Day the men of Nineveh will be raised up
> and stand next to this people
> and they will condemn this people.
> Why?
> Because when Jonah preached they repented,
> and there is something greater than Jonah here.
> (Luke 11:29–32)

You both sit there for a while, watching people.

Enter the presence of God and ask that your image of Jesus not be distorted but true. "Let me run the risk of knowing him as he was and is."

Chapter Twenty

The people are not going to be saved by his preaching of the good news. In trying to wake up the devout to their danger he asks a question: "You serpents, brood of vipers, how can you escape being condemned to hell?" (Matt. 23:33 NJB). It sounds like a rhetorical question—"You really cannot escape hell"—but it isn't. For Jesus it is a real question, it is now the central question of his life. The path he has been following was designed to help this people escape from being condemned to hell. It is for this purpose that God sends the prophets. "This is why—look—I am sending you prophets" (Matt. 23:33 NJB).

This is the goal of all God's activity in human history. Now the path that leads to that goal is blocked. After all that has been done, how can the chosen people escape being condemned to hell? Jesus is faced with the need to choose. Is he to live out his days with a God who cannot deliver his people?

Not only is his mission in ruins, but any alternative way of rescuing the people seems eliminated because Jesus sees that he himself will be stopped soon no matter what he does. His life itself is now a threat that the righteous leaders feel justified in bringing to an end. The messiah will soon become helpless and be put to death.

But Jesus still has a choice. He can choose to believe that God will find a way, even though there now is little evidence for it. A text he has in his heart becomes his choice.

> But I shall look to the LORD,
> my hope is in the God who will save me;
> my God will hear me. (Mic. 7:7 NJB)

He had already recalled the verses just before this one to describe how his mission would reveal the animosities present even in the family. The verse after this one is now pertinent too:

> Do not gloat over me, my enemy:
> though I have fallen, I shall rise;
> though I live in darkness,
> the LORD is my light. (Mic. 7:8 NJB)

He has a choice. The collapse of his mission of preaching reveals a likelihood that human freedom with its power of final decision is going to prevent God's desire from being accomplished. But Jesus can ignore the appearances and trust that God—who is even more concerned about this turn of events, and even more determined—will find a way.

Jesus is feeling his way forward into a great secret.

This mood is captured well in a parable he used earlier. A man sows wheat in his field. But while people sleep an enemy sows weeds among the wheat. The two seeds go to work secretly, both quite small and unimpressive and working unseen beneath the soil. They grow day by day, and finally they come above ground, wheat and weeds. It is only when they appear that the owner realizes that he has an enemy who is determined to ruin the harvest. "Some enemy has done this" (Matt. 13:28 NJB). How can the harvest be saved anyway? Or is all lost? Jesus imagines the laborers saying to the owner, "Do you want us to go and weed it out?" But he said no (Matt. 13:28–29 NJB).

This same awareness is now present in Jesus. There will be no easy solution, and although the people will, of course, be saved—is not God God?—it cannot be done painlessly, by a word. "No, because when you pull up the weeds you might pull up the wheat with it" (Matt. 13:29).

It is a vision of human nature: weeds and wheat in everyone. No one will be left if you weed thoroughly. Each person is a tangle of both. The child is wrapped round with a python, all tangled up. You cannot strike at the snake with a machete, you may strike off an arm. The two seeds are both at work in each person, the yeast of God leading to faith and love, and the yeast of hypocrisy leading to dishonesty and selfishness. They must be separated, of course,

126

but it will not be simple. Nothing simple will work. Nothing that has ever been heard of will do the job. The only thing that will work will amaze everyone.

> So many nations will be astonished
> and kings will stay tight-lipped before him,
> seeing what had never been told them,
> learning what they had not heard before. (Isa. 52:15 NJB)

For God has a way. What is it? A way that has been hidden since the foundation of the world. Now it will be revealed. What is it like to sense that you are being led into the secret that is at the heart of the new age?

Certain things are clear. Jesus knows he is at the center of the secret. Whatever is to happen and however it is to happen, he will be its centerpiece. He feels assured of that. Somehow, through him, God will reach his goal. He is the bridegroom.

And another thing is very clear: He will soon be put to death. Somehow his being put to death will become the salvation of all. How can that be? We are so accustomed to the notion of redemption that we easily miss how alien that notion is, how unbelievable — even now — it is, how it violates our sense of the seriousness of each individual's life. It breaks the iron rules of the game of existence. "Who has given credence to what we have heard? And who has seen in it a revelation of the LORD's arm?" (Isa. 53:1 NJB).

That someone else's life can be the meaning of my life, that it can be given to me as a gift, this is difficult not so much to explain or understand but to believe. It is resisted by the deepest levels of the personality even while it is being understood.

That your life and example can inspire me, that we do believe. That your advice and your arm, and your affection, can help me, that we see. But in each case it is a help and an inspiration for me to make the critical choice, to use my freedom. But in redemption my very choice is being given to me as a gift. This choice of mine has come into the possession of someone else, and he kindly offers it to me as a gift. It is precisely the free choice that I need, and in its being given to me it delivers me.

This is the vision that is entering into Jesus' consciousness: a suggestion that all of human history will be based on his life and his decisions. What is it like as this begins to dawn upon him? How does it feel to become conscious of an invitation from what is most profound and most holy within his experience, an invitation to believe that this people will indeed be saved and that he is God's salvation for them.

Perhaps a parable will help us glimpse what it is like for Jesus as he moves into the redemptive decision of God, the secret hidden for ages.

We are all money lenders. And great borrowers ourselves. Suddenly the government announces all debts are canceled. Some are delighted — those who owed more than they had actually lent. But I am amazed. I lent a huge fortune, all I had, and I never borrowed a cent. I own nothing. I am ruined.

It's basically unfair. Nothing is more plain. Such an intervention will destroy the money market. The fear that it will happen again will mean that nobody will be willing to lend.

Let's try a variation where everyone will be delighted. In this variation everyone has borrowed much more than they have lent. Impossible! Right. So we'll make an exception. One man and one man only has lent huge amounts and he has borrowed nothing. All the others, though, have lent very little and have borrowed heavily.

Now the government steps in. Everyone is delighted. Except for the one man, unless he happens to be the government and has made the decision.

"So he let them both off."
(Luke 7:42 NJB)

Jesus imagines such a scenario. It produces great joy and love. Nobody complains about the unfairness of it, because the only person who is being treated unfairly is the one who makes the decision. All the rules are changed, the iron laws that we all acknowledge. Your life's meaning must come from your own use of your freedom. Now your own use of your freedom is coming to you as a gift from someone else's life and meaning.

The day of reckoning, the day when all the loans are called in, will be a day when a spectacular goodness will be revealed.

Somehow in his dying Jesus will accomplish this event. This is what Jesus is beginning to sense. There are texts available to him. They have not been so important up to now. He memorized them years before, but it is only now that they come alive in his consciousness as he searches for God's will. He recalls Isaiah:

> He was despised, the lowest of men,
> a man of sorrows, familiar with suffering,
> one from whom, as it were, we averted our gaze,
> despised, for whom we had no regard.
> Yet ours were the sufferings he was bearing. (Isa. 53:3–4 NJB)

The sufferings of one person would be suffered instead by another. Is it possible? There will indeed be a handing over to torturers. Instead of the unforgiving being "handed over to the torturers" (Matt. 18:34), it is Jesus himself who will be handed over.

It's like a new kind of medicine: I break an arm, but if I then go and bruise your arm, mine will be healed. It really makes no sense.

> We thought of him as someone being punished
> and struck with afflictions by God;
> whereas he was being wounded for our rebellions,
> crushed because of our guilt. (Isa. 53:4–5 NJB)

So this is the messiah that God has had in mind all along. That is what comes into Jesus' consciousness as an invitation from God. Something God has thought up at the depths of divine reality. God has thought of it first. "The punishment reconciling us fell on him, and we have been healed by his bruises" (Isa. 53:5 NJB).

There it is — the bruises of one heal another. "If he gives his life as a sin offering . . . through him the LORD's good pleasure will be done" (Isa. 53:10 NJB).

There will indeed be a saving of this people. But it will take a form undreamed of. No one had ever imagined it. "My servant will justify many by taking their guilt on himself" (Isa. 53:11 NJB).

> Because he poured out his soul to death,
> and was numbered with the transgressors;
> yet he bore the sin of many
> and made intercession for the transgressors.
> (Isa. 53:12 RSV)

How can the death of anyone mean so much? It is in this invitation to let himself be put to death that a question arises: The messiah, who is he? What is his true dignity? Of what dignity is he that by his dying he saves the human flock?

The question of his own identity is present with Jesus throughout his life but never at the center of his attention. Center stage is occupied by his search for the Father's will. Only gradually does the other question comes forward, forced by the peculiar nature of the act that will bring salvation.

He sees himself as the centerpiece in the coming of the Kingdom, God's final entry into human life. He will judge the nations. There is a text where we glimpse Jesus in the midst of his searching.

> While the Pharisees were gathered round,
> Jesus put to them this question,
> "What is your opinion about the Christ?
> Whose son is he?" (Matt. 22:41–42 NJB)

He has discovered a verse in the Psalms that raises some interesting possibilities as he wonders about the true dignity of the messiah, one whose death could have such meaning.

The Pharisees give the usual answer: the messiah is David's son. Then Jesus recalls the text, the first verse of Psalm 110:

> The LORD declared to my Lord,
> take your seat at my right hand,
> till I have made your enemies
> your footstool. (Matt. 22:44 NJB)

In the text the first "LORD" refers to Yahweh, and the second "Lord" refers to the messiah, and David is the author—at least this was what everyone believed in Jesus' day. This means that David is saying that "Yahweh declared to the messiah, my Lord." There's the problem: David is calling the messiah his Lord. Jesus points up the problem: "If David calls him Lord, how can he be his son?" (Matt. 22:45 NJB).

His question could not be answered.

Does it suggest to Jesus that David can call the messiah Lord because while being his son, he is also of a dignity far loftier than David himself? This is not such a surprising question for someone exploring the strange nature of God's saving act—how it involves one man and, even then, his dying.

Somehow his death will be God canceling all debts.

How capable is any human mind of receiving the assurance of redemption through the death of one special man? There are those who hold that this awareness can come only by evolving over a long period of time. But I agree with those who see Jesus himself as the origin of this central aspect of our faith.

What is it like to be at the center of such an invasion of human history? Remember, it is a human being who is experiencing this. He is in possession of Scripture. His heart is moved with a desire to save this people from the destruction he sees threatening them. He chooses not to take the appearances of failure as a sign of God's indifference or weakness. He chooses to believe that God's involvement is total. In this context, a text like the passage from Isaiah 53 resonates with great power.

With the awareness of his approaching death, a tension enters Jesus' life. An edge to his words appears that is not present in the Resurrection events. He expresses it vividly: "I have come to bring fire to the earth, and how I wish it was blazing already" (Luke 12:49 NJB).

That image of fire was a favorite of the Baptist. Now, with the sureness of his death, it enters into Jesus' speech. Here he uses it to describe an anxiety, a nervous anticipation. He has a task to perform and he badly wants to get on with it. He is describing his own eagerness to move forward into God's will.

We use the term *baptism of fire*. It's what a person who is new on the job has to undergo. It tests whether all the training that has preceded will be of any real use. Jesus calls his torture and death a baptism. "There is a baptism I must still receive" (Luke 12:50 NJB).

It is an image of a coming passivity in the face of some sort of assault. He expresses his feelings: "How much stress I am under until it is all done" (Luke 12:50). He is being drawn into God's will: a painful death from which he shrinks and an escape from disaster for his brothers and sisters, which draws him forward.

On another occasion he uses a different image to describe his coming death: "Can you drink the cup that I shall drink?" (Mark 10:38 NJB).

He is in a state of extreme tension, and he describes it well. A cup is being extended to him by God, and he experiences both repulsion and intense desire. Part of his repulsion is physical. But part is a sense of the unfairness of what is about to take place. Just as it had been with the Elijah—what a disgrace! The Elijah was taken prisoner and then had his head cut off at the wish of a dancing girl. Now his own head will be pressed down, submerged, and his enemies will gloat. They will appear victorious. His own followers will be shocked, and alone.

It is a time when he hears more and more clearly God's invitation. And it is a time of great temptation. A struggle is taking place within as he comes to his decision. He is aware of his own freedom to choose. God is issuing an invitation, not an order. He is free. God will rescue him if he asks. But it is clear, God wants him not to ask. And he chooses that.

But Satan has been at work and still is. Jesus must be persuaded to refuse. There are excellent reasons for refusing. Why should any further effort be made to save such hypocrites? The temptations concern the choice to love. He is the elder brother, and he is being asked to suffer in the place of the wicked one.

It is no wonder then that when he begins to tell all this to his apostles, he is so upset at Peter's words "This must not happen to you" (Matt. 16:22 NJB). These are Satan's words! Jesus is reaching his decision only by steeling himself willfully to do it, and Peter opens up the struggle all over again. He is not going to go through this again, now with Peter in the place of Satan. He makes it plain: the decision is taken; this is the future they are heading toward if they stay with him. "You are an obstacle in my path" (Matt. 16:23 NJB). God himself has been inviting Jesus down this path. Jesus is letting God's very thoughts and desires and plans enter. "You are thinking not as God thinks but as human beings do" (Matt. 16:23 NJB). Jesus is glimpsing what God is thinking, and he chooses to be open to it. But it is so different from what human beings think. Somehow the collapse of his mission will serve God's purposes better than its apparent success.

Much earlier, when the disciples return from their first mission, Jesus points up the danger of resting on appearances. It is easy to do and instinctive, and it appears to be quite harmless.

The seventy-two came back rejoicing.
"Lord," they said, "even the devils submit to us
when we use your name." (Luke 10:17 NJB)

What could be more natural? If they didn't have this joy at their evident success, we would wonder about their normality. It's so evidently harmless. But Jesus steps in, quite deliberately. "Do not rejoice that the spirits submit to you" (Luke 10:20 NJB).

Why not? This way of living is faithless. Here we see the Kingdom succeeding, here we see a setback. Now we are elated, now set down a bit. No. It's all living apart from faith! Even the successes are apart from faith. The source of this joy and this sorrow is not what is really happening but appearances. Once Satan hooks you on appearances, you will lead a life apart from faith.

What then? Is the life of the apostles to be terminal glumness? Not at all! But their rejoicing will be based on reality. And because it is based on the real, it cannot be taken away by appearances. If I enjoy the successes, I will be depressed at the failures. But if I believe, I will be happy regardless of success or failure. So he tells them, "Rejoice instead that your names are written in heaven" (Luke 10:20 NJB).

This is the basis of the believer's joy—an event he himself has had nothing to do with. A kindly act of Someone Else. Getting to know that Other is the joy we are invited into. God's spectacular kindly personality will be a cause of endless joy. Start to taste it now. You cannot live at both levels. You cannot take your joy from reality and from appearance. If you try to do it, reality will get lost.

Get to know God and the inner beauty of the divine person and no one will be able to take away your joy. Be aware of God's decisions and you will be drawn into admiring God. You will instinctively bless the heavenly Father.

I bless you, Father,
Lord of heaven and earth,
for hiding these things from the learned and the clever
and revealing them to little children. (Luke 10:21 NJB)

The faith experience is most profound when the Spirit floods the soul with joy at the marvelous personality of God. We delight at the choices God makes: "Yes, Father, for that is what it has pleased you to do" (Luke 10:21 NJB). Unless you learn this new path to joy, you shall be ever caught in the ups and downs of the appearances of success and failure. It is the clever who rest on their evident success. But hidden from them is the knowledge of the spectacular decision of God: the Father writes names in heaven, and that is what counts. This is true whether you are in the midst of apparent success or failure, and only the children will ever understand. The children understand because in their helplessness their eyes are fixed on the Father's power and kindness.

It is the devout who are so aware of their successes. They use their evident success to persuade everyone of the holiness of their lives. It is to them that Jesus spells out the sharp contrast between the thinking-as-God-thinks and the thinking-as-humans-think that he condemns in Peter. "What is highly esteemed in human eyes is loathsome in the sight of God" (Luke 16:15 NJB).

But is it really so harmful to rejoice at a successful mission?

This path leads to the rejection of a dying messiah. It is this "harmless" choice that blossoms in Judas. That yeast, the very yeast he sees at work in the leaders, is at work among his own. Their very rejoicing in success will leave them helpless in defeat. How will they survive as they watch him humiliated if they are still hooked on apparent success? They must be prepared.

> Then, taking the twelve aside,
> he said to them,
> "Look, we are going up to Jerusalem,
> and everything that is written by the prophets
> about the Son of Man
> is to come true." (Luke 18:31 NJB)

But even in this he feels no confidence. They offer him no evidence that he is getting through.

> They could make nothing of this;
> what he said was quite obscure to them,
> they did not understand what he was telling them.
> (Luke 18:34 NJB)

Even here he has to trust that despite the evident uselessness of trying, God is at work within them and not ineffectively.

134

Prayer Exercise

Each of us has an image of Jesus that enters our prayer. It can be very different from the images we find in the Gospels. For many people Jesus comes through as though he were just another apostle. For some he is nothing more than an assuring presence.

But peculiar to the Gospel Jesus and at the heart of his personality is a conviction he has: "People need to hear me tell them things: I am the word."

He has a piece of news that can help people deal with their past. He knows people need to hear what he can tell them about the future. Most important, he has information that can transform their present experience.

Is your image of Jesus that of a good, wise apostle?

Is Jesus more an assuring presence in your prayer, or has he a message for you?

Are you experiencing what the apostles experienced: being completely known and being completely forgiven? Does the image of Jesus in your prayer produce a similar intensity?

Jesus is not just an assuring presence. He was a man with a message, and that type of person can be very obnoxious. But he knew that it was crucial for people to hear what he had to say.

The content of his message was beyond any apostle's creating. It was hidden from all until Jesus spoke. "I will reveal what has been hidden since the foundation of the world."

Jesus sees us weighed down by our past, even when we are not aware of it. Guilt cripples us, especially our unlove. *"Your sins are forgiven."*

We may ignore the threats the future holds, especially the threat of death, but we are not thereby freed from the paralysis produced by anxiety. *"I will raise you up."*

Our inability here and now to fulfill the love command will, if we face it honestly, tempt us to despair. *"I will send the Holy Spirit."*

(Living water, the power to love, God's own kingly power, the Kingdom of Heaven.)

When we pray each day, God is wanting to speak to our guilt, our anxiety, and especially our despair. It is the hearing of that voice that fills our life with a joy no one can take from us.

Chapter Twenty-One

Jesus' mission is collapsing. He is certain that he will soon be silenced. He knows that the disciples are baffled at the thought of a dying Messiah. It is unwelcome to them. No matter how clearly and powerfully he expresses it, nothing appears to be clicking within them.

So much needs to be said, and there is no time to say it. "I still have many things to say to you but they would be too much for you to bear now" (John 16:12 NJB).

In this situation Jesus makes a critical decision, one not dictated by Scripture at all. It springs from his own choosing and from his creativity. It gives us a unique opportunity to see his inner self at work.

He decides to enter into the world of ritual. It comes totally from within his own personality. At some point the decision strikes him with great force. He must do it. It is a rare instance where his freedom is without any clear leads.

At the beginning of his ministry people came to him asking to be cured, although there was no clear call for working miracles in the Scriptures. He was astonished by their initiative.

> "Do you believe I can do this?"
> They said, "Lord, we do."
> Then he touched their eyes, saying,
> "According to your faith
> let it be done to you." (Matt. 9:28–29 NJB)

He read someone else's initiative as an invitation from God to work a miracle. It was their childlike faith that set the miracle going.

But in moving into ritual, only his own initiative is at work. He feels it is important, critically important. So often in subsequent centuries people have found it not quite necessary. It doesn't seem to be a part of the heart of his gospel. He can be grasped in all his fullness without the ritual. So much so that for many Christians he is seen as not initiating a ritual at all.

But for Jesus the ritual he initiates is somehow the primary path of coming to know him and his gospel. In the ritual Jesus places an emphasis that is hard for us to understand and explain. Although Jesus' message may seem to be much cleaner, much more coherent and logical, without the ritual, Jesus deliberately involves himself and his followers in it. He quite deliberately muddies the waters. He forces us to focus where the intellect is least at home. He places at the very center of our believing something for our imagination and our senses.

His message is so totally spiritual. What can it have to do with the clumsiness of ritual? Doesn't he see that this would lead to endless confusion and to a cheapening of his simple vision?

Still he feels now that without ritual his message will not be heard, that it can be understood only through a ritual presentation. Only a ritual can communicate the mysterious nature of God's secret. Only a ritual can keep drawing people to focus on the secret and spectacular deed of God. It is ritual that will be understood by the simple and the unlearned, the children, even as it is being misinterpreted by the clever.

In any event, he makes a decision. He embodies the core of his gospel in a ritual act. It is in line with his emphasis on images. For Jesus the struggle between the two seeds and the two yeasts is taking place within the human imagination. He will invade the imagination with a symbol that is also real. It will vivify the "already" nature of the Kingdom. Through his faith and in the reality contained by the image, the believer will be already there, the Kingdom will be already present within him.

This deliberate decision of Jesus provides us with a powerful and fresh look at the good news itself. For Jesus the good news lends itself to ritual expression. Just as he sees in it a reality that can best—if not only—be conveyed by parables and images, so too he sees it as ideally presented in a ritual communication.

What is it about the gospel that finds its fullness of expression in ritual? Traditionally the central emphasis of ritual is on the fact that God's initiative is at work. How better to get across the supreme importance of what God is doing than to embody it in a ritual where the believer is thoroughly passive? Something is being done to him, and that is the facet of the good news that, while being quite easy to understand and explain, is most easy not to believe and realize.

We are back at that moment when Jesus warns the disciples away from false joy. It is the learned and the clever who will be caught up with success and failure, with human efforts. It is the child, the helpless, who places all her joy in the good news that God has written her name down in heaven. How better to preach this word than to bring people to a ritual? There they are fed with a food beyond all human purchasing, beyond all human worthiness.

How convinced he is of his own importance at this moment. He makes himself the center of the ritual. He is by now seeing himself as a more-than-human figure. This first-century carpenter whose mission is collapsing and whose life itself is all but over feels pressured to find a way to rescue his followers from the ruins. It is the simple ritual in the quiet of the upper room—to all appearances a dinner for has-beens and destroyed hopes. He insists on initiating them into a ritual. It has a powerful impact on them. They are watching a man who has no grounds for hope act and speak as if his own plans are surely coming to fulfillment. Jesus is in the full flush of assurance.

He is caught up in what will be happening to them within the next few hours. The movement will go under first. Its leader will be dead, its members scattered. Everything will be submerged. It is the baptism. There will be no signs of life. It will be the hour of darkness. His apostles will have no reason to believe. He can see it coming—how it will shake them, how they will fail, how they will feel.

What will happen to them, his closest friends? How will they survive? It comes to him in a recollection of Zechariah:

> Awake, sword, against my shepherd,
> against the man who is close to me—
> declares the LORD of Hosts! (Zech. 13:7 NJB)

A strange occurrence—God is calling for a sword to be used against the chosen one. Even in the midst of the enemy's might, trust! The Lord will be using it for his own goal. "Strike the shepherd, scatter the sheep!" (Zech. 13:7 NJB). They will scatter in confusion. Despite his warnings that these things would occur, still they will be unprepared for them. Only a third will survive.

> I shall pass this third through the fire,
> refine them as silver is refined,
> test them as gold is tested. (Zech. 13:9 NJB)

Does Jesus wonder how many of his apostles will fall away? Will eight or nine of them fall away? Certainly Judas. It was so plain to him and painful.

> It is not an enemy who taunts me —
>   then I could bear it;
> it is not an adversary who deals insolently with me —
>   then I could hide from him.
> But it is you, my equal,
> my companion, my familiar friend.
> We used to hold sweet converse together;
> within God's house we walked in fellowship.
> (Ps. 55:12–14, RSV)

What were the conversations of Jesus and Judas? How does Jesus feel as this man he is bound to hardens himself against him and blunts any effort at reconciliation? "One of you is about to betray me, one of you eating with me" (Mark 14:18 NJB). Jesus reminds Judas, who is still present at the supper, of what their friendship had once been. He refers to Psalm 41, a sufferer who has been deserted:

> And when one comes to see me, he utters empty words,
> while his heart gathers mischief;
> when he goes out, he tells it abroad.
> Even my bosom friend in whom I trusted,
> who ate of my bread,
> has lifted his heel against me. (Ps. 41:6–7, 9 RSV)

He will be kissed by this former friend. What a moment of pain for Jesus. His friend is in terrible trouble and hardened against any help. This can be so much more painful than physical pain. Sometimes our heart's pain is so great we deliberately inflict physical pain on ourselves to act as an outlet, an escape, a distraction. Does Jesus go through his passion with his attention riveted on the loss of this bosom friend, mercifully distracted by the torturers? Judas's life is coming to a fullness of freedom. He is about to become himself. With the golden opportunity that comes from living in the generation of the messiah comes the opportunity to betray him. The gift is double-edged. Jesus makes people whom he draws into his friendship capable of unspeakable evils.

He tries to deliver the apostles from their illusions. The moment has come for the messiah to go his way alone. No one will be there to support him. This is the nature of salvation: one alone saves, the only one who does not need to be redeemed. All of the others are passive, part of the problem. But Peter will have none of this image of himself. "I will lay down my life for you" (John 13:37 NAB). Jesus sounds painfully aware that there is little he can do in the face of such illusion. These words are meant to comfort him, but he knows how unreal they are. He is being offered nothing but illusion. "*You* will lay down your life for *me,* will you?" (John 13:38 NAB). Peter has it upside down. What he will do for Jesus, the usual human image. What I do for God—that is what counts. It is so ironic here, just as God is about to be most active for humanity.

Later the apostles offer him consoling words: "We believe that you came from God" (John 16:30 NJB). He is so conscious of the illusion. Their faith is so shallow. There is so little he can do about it now. "Do you believe at last?" (John 16:31 NJB).

Then he delivers to them the truth about their faith.

> Listen, the time will come—
> indeed it has come already—
> when you are going to be scattered,
> each going his own way
> and leaving me alone. (John 16:32 NJB)

But it is too late to hope that anything he says will make a difference. He is left with no real evidence of any success. The ruin is everywhere—the Pharisees, the people, and his own disciples. They are the very image of a failed mission.

141

Prayer Exercise

Move slowly through this, a step at a time.

Jesus is tired from teaching in the temple all day. He sits down opposite the treasury and watches the people. The disciples are scattered about, some sitting, some standing in small groups, chatting or resting. You watch the crowds in the temple court coming and going.

Take time observing the crowd. Now you notice a peculiar face, now an odd dress or a color combination, now a little family. Typical bystanding. You wonder what's going on inside of this one or that one. Make up a likely answer. There's a man all alone, waiting for someone. Who? He's very restless.

You turn your eyes and watch Jesus for a while. He is looking at the crowds, going from person to person. His eyes stop. You look around to see what holds his attention. It's a typical man, about thirty-five, nicely dressed but not wealthy. He is leaving the temple with his father and his son. Now he is out of sight. Jesus looks at another, a very ordinary character. And so on.

You notice that John has left Jesus' side. There is a space open so you go over and sit there. Jesus looks at you and asks, "What do you think? Will any of them be saved?" He's so serious. You talk together.

Jesus then says, "What a catastrophe — to be part of this generation. This generation will receive the messiah and kill him. If I had not come, if I had not spoken to them, they would have been blameless; but as it is, they have no excuse for their sin."

> If I had not performed such works among them
> as no one else has ever done,
> they would be blameless;
> but as it is, they have seen all this
> and still they hate both me and my Father.
> (John 15:24 JB)

There is more conversation. He then recites Ps. 35:19 JB.

Do not let my lying enemies gloat over me,
do not let those who hate me for no reason
exchange sly glances.

Then Ps. 69:4 JB.

> More people hate me for no reason
> than I have hairs on my head.
> More are groundlessly hostile
> than I have hair to show.

You both sit there in silence looking at the people.

You continue to watch. You look at one person carefully. You hear someone weeping. It is Jesus. He speaks:

> Jerusalem! Jerusalem!
> You kill the prophets and stone those sent to you!
> How often have I longed to gather your children
> as a hen gathers her chicks under her wings,
> and you refuse.
> So be it! Your house will be left desolate!
> (Matt. 23:37–38 JB)

Enter God's presence. Ask for the courage to face the real Jesus with his challenges and his insistent call to leave your comfortable illusions. Journey with him into the truth about yourself and your great need for him.

Chapter Twenty-Two

At the supper the failure of his mission becomes most apparent and vivid in one awful scene, a scene of such unacceptable behavior that it has never been portrayed by an artist. There are so many paintings of these last hours of Jesus, but no one has ever depicted this awful moment of truth.

Jesus makes clear that he is leaving them. Who will take his place? They actually get into an argument! This competitiveness had produced similar scenes before, but Jesus was swift to correct them. He had described the behavior of unbelievers, and how they covet power.

> You know that among the gentiles
> the rulers lord it over them,
> and great men make their authority felt.
> (Matt. 20:25 NJB)

He has heard and seen how humans behave. It is a pattern of behavior based on illusion. It makes sense only if you do not hear the good news. Once you hear the good news, that type of behaving makes no sense. "It cannot be like that with you" (Matt. 20:26 NAB).

Such behavior is a clear sign of unbelief. The whole point of belief is that a divine event has occurred within God, a decision has been made by God, and it is of such a spectacular nature that striving for power is no longer meaningful. Grasping the good news destroys all thirst for power. Where there is still a power struggle, the good news is being ignored.

It's just like the refusal to forgive, a sure sign that the gospel is being rejected, the news has not been heard. The apostles mustn't end up the same as unbelievers. Jesus had spoken out forcefully.

144

On another occasion he had called a little child into the group. He warned them: Only children enter the Kingdom. Those who seek power cannot enter.

The apostles had been impressed. Their ambitions went underground. But now how can it be avoided? A new leader to succeed Jesus has to be chosen quickly. They begin imagining a future without him. "A dispute arose among them about who should be regarded as the greatest" (Luke 22:24 NAB). The word for dispute can be translated more literally as "a love of winning," a willingness to have it out with somebody, urged by the desire to score off them. Others are used to reveal my superiority. I stand up for my rights. After all, why should he be allowed to walk off with it?

Competitiveness comes roaring up out of its hiding place. It involves abusive language—that's the kind of dispute meant by the Greek word. Someone uses the word *fool*. The enemy who has sowed the weeds in the field is now letting his power be displayed. Right here at the supper Jesus is being invited to see the ineffectiveness of his work.

It is hard for us to imagine what a horror this is to Jesus. We have a remarkable tolerance for this kind of behavior. We understand its reasons. We do it ourselves. Had one of the apostles become somewhat drunk, we would be more offended. Had one of them grabbed a serving girl and started to assault her sexually, we would be shocked. But the disciples' arguing doesn't have that effect on us. We have a remarkable tolerance for disputing. We would find it much more offensive if someone had emptied his nostrils into the wine jar.

But for Jesus this is the most shocking of all. His own closest followers are being sifted like wheat by Satan. He prays for them, especially for Peter. Peter has the best claim of all for the leadership. Jesus himself singled him out. But Peter is full of his own virtue. It is clear to Peter that he is not like the rest of them. Well, it is in the hands of God.

While the apostles are caught up in a power struggle over the future Kingdom, Jesus hears the suggestion that it has all been wasted. What a horror for him to watch, to watch quietly, as all the rest lose interest in him. He becomes the unobserved as the heat of the argument intensifies. How does he feel as they squabble? There is no child around to bring forward. What should he do?

He had once imagined the strange kind of master God is. When he arrives late in the night from a long journey, he takes the apron off the servant who has waited up for him, ties it around his own waist, forces the servant to sit, and waits upon her.

John describes this supper moment as one of intense awareness for Jesus, a full consciousness of living in two worlds, this world that he is about to pass from and the world where God dwells.

> Jesus knew that the Father had put everything
> into his hands,
> and that he had come from God
> and was returning to God. (John 13:3 NJB).

He becomes the master of his own parable. This is the way God does his ruling. He puts on an apron. It is that God-as-servant image, and there is resistance. God must not behave like this. Such a God undermines much of what we consider to be reasonable human behavior. It especially undermines the reasonableness behind the dispute over who is number one.

If the job description for a superior of a religious community included washing the dishes after each meal, cleaning the bathrooms, and keeping the corridors and public rooms polished and dusted, it would have quite an impact on our ambition.

> If anyone wants to be first,
> he must make himself last of all
> and servant of all. (Mark 9:35 NJB)

Oddly enough this happens to be the good news. Power has become our servant. Those who need it will receive God's energy to work for them. But this news has no home in the hearts of his closest followers.

Among them the infection is great. Each apostle's enemies are being revealed, and they are members of his own household. Jesus' coming exposes the secrets of their hearts: their competitiveness is in plain view.

In the face of this infection gripping those he loves, God becomes a doctor, and Jesus sees himself as God as doctor in the world. Now by his decision to involve his followers in a ritual, Jesus makes himself into a medicine. God becomes medicine.

146

The contrast between God and human beings is at its sharpest. Peter's determination is to be the leader. Powerful resistance grips the other apostles, and God desires to free Peter from this ambition. The complete lack of ambition that Jesus reveals to be God is now being made available to us.

The apostles drink his blood and eat his flesh. Jesus will be their only meaning. Apart from what comes to them through him, there will be nothing of value in their lives. The foundation of their lives will be a gift, and he is that gift.

Whatever awareness he may have of his personal identity at this point, his human mind is seeing itself as the pivot of every human life in a way that nothing merely human could ever be. Who can give his own flesh and blood as food and drink? We are in the world of imagination again, and Jesus invents an unparalleled symbol, and quite deliberately.

What does he think he is doing? What kind of self-awareness is implied in creating such a symbol? Are there previous moments that led up to this, steps that are hidden from us, such as the suggestion in chapter 6 of John's Gospel about the bread of life? We have the finished product. But we know that, like the parables, there has been a process that flowers into the action and words of the supper. A parallel question developed step by step with it. The question of the dignity of Jesus' personality: Who is he?

How strange that the flowering takes such a specific form! It is not inevitable. Nor does it seem obvious that this ritual was necessary. But what we do have is a concrete moment filled with most peculiar particulars, the products of Jesus' human choosing. His unique personality is center stage. His mark is on this moment. It is impossible to forget these strange words and gestures and the terrible importance that he attaches to them. In that dark night when the mission is about to go under, Jesus takes time to do something he considers of utter importance.

If we could see it all afresh and capture this decision of Jesus in its freedom, it would be a source of great insight into what makes him the person he is. But to us it has the appearance of an inevitable way of passing time at the last supper. To the apostles, and to Jesus himself, there is no obviousness at all, only decisions coming from the deepest level of his freedom.

The ritual he chooses expresses human helplessness. The apostles are asked to let themselves be fed by the new manna. The new life, the new Kingdom will be theirs through a being fed—like babies. They are invited to become little children, to open their mouths and let God feed them on bread come down from heaven.

It is not the way we imagine getting close to God. We put our trust in our service. It's as if God has a sign out, Servant Needed, and we must get up the courage to be willing to take the job. It could be a very difficult job. But we are determined to do the best we can. And in this way we will get close to our "boss."

We will do God favors, and God will be in our debt. He will notice us and remember us. We will be on his list for a very nice Christmas tip.

We will serve at God's table. When he is hungry, he will tell us, and we will get him a fine steak.

We will please him by our offerings. "If I am hungry I shall not tell you" (Ps. 50:12 NJB). How can we serve him if he won't cooperate? "I will not accept any bullock from your homes" (Ps. 50:9). What about the sacrifices we want to offer? If they do not get us close to God, what does? "Let thanksgiving be your sacrifice to God" (Ps. 50:14 NJB).

But thanksgiving is given to one who does the favor. If our sacrifice is that we are to be thanking God, we must be conscious of God's favors to us, of his service to us. It is only when we experience God washing away our dirt and healing our infection and feeding our open mouth that we will be able to offer true sacrifice: thanksgiving.

In the Eucharist symbol Jesus casts the human being as a child, an infected one, and God as the doctor and the medicine. He did not have to ritualize at all. In inventing a particular liturgy, he is quite free. That he did choose to ritualize is not surprising. It fits his decision to preach in parables. It brings the image to a peak of intensity. The particular form of the rite he uses to express himself carries the core of his gospel message within its simple words and gestures. The Eucharist is most revealing of what Jesus thought he was doing, and who he thought he was. It is a unique self-expression in human history, and it reveals a consciousness quite aware of its own uniqueness.

Prayer Exercise

Imagine each step as you go.

Imagine yourself invisible and sitting, watching a scene of abject poverty or suffering. Starving Ethiopian children and their parents; a refugee camp in Asia; a leper colony; a street in Calcutta.

People are moving about, real people. Watch them as they walk by you. Notice how they are dressed, and look at some of the faces. Notice where they are looking and how this person has a peculiar walk.

Where is he coming from? Make up a likely answer. Where is he going? Try another person. What is she so obviously afraid of? What is the one hope left to her now? What are her real chances for any change? Try four or five more. Let them come alive in your imagination.

Close your eyes and just listen to the noises for a while. What are you feeling? Do you feel repelled? attracted? comfortable?

Notice that there is someone else watching the scene with you. It is the heavenly Father. Watch the Father as people pass. Follow God's eyes as they go from one person to another. What is the Father's reaction to this scene? What is God's reaction to this person, to that one? How does God feel about what this person is thinking or what that person is worried about?

What could the Father do about this scene that isn't already being done? Would you want God to work some miracles, multiplying loaves or healing?

Notice how life goes on. God does nothing dramatic.

Imagine that in the crowd you suddenly recognize the face of a relative very close to you. How do you feel as you watch this person in such a place? Would you want God to work some miracle to help?

I am drawn to ignore the needy and to see myself filled with compassion and to ignore the compassionate love filling the Father's heart.

In prayer to God the Father, ask for the gift of honesty. Let the Lord reveal to you how you rehearse your good deeds and how you remember the faults of others, how much you rely on an image of yourself as a generous person. Let God reveal to you how automatic are your evaluations of the motives of others and their level of selfishness.

Let that part of you come to the surface, that part which is kept hidden and which makes you resemble the elder brother of the prodigal son.

"Lord, give me the gift of knowing myself as others know me, and as you know me—the truth that leads to complete freedom."

Chapter Twenty-Three

Repeatedly in his public career Jesus is faced with the problem of evil: How can God be so good when he does nothing about human suffering? He had to face this in his own heart first. He had chosen to reject the conclusion that God has no concern for us. God's unconcern is only apparent, on the surface.

Jesus deliberately chooses over and over again to believe that in reality God is already totally active, like a shepherd pursuing a lost sheep. This is what is really occurring at the deepest levels hidden from the human eye. Of course God is doing something. If you knew God, you would know that.

But we must remember that his knowledge of God was by choice and through faith. He faced the same evidence we face, and for him as for us the question was not settled by that evidence. Jesus himself chose to believe.

This choice is what most identifies him as a person. He comes to be an unshakable decision to trust the Father. His human consciousness grows more and more into the consciousness of a son, a refusal to doubt the Father's love no matter what the appearances are.

As his public career begins to disintegrate, he has any signs of God's love for him and God's power for him taken away. The evidence that God really is with him is disappearing. He has not depended on that evidence anyway. He has warned his disciples not to rest on their apparent successes. So when these superficial signs of God's favors are removed, Jesus still chooses to believe.

He has taught people not to be taken in by appearances. When God seems most distant, he is actually most involved. God works like a seed in the ground—hidden but effective.

Now the moment arrives when for Jesus there is no evidence at all. After so many leave him, now his closest followers are about to abandon him. They revealed at the supper how effectively Satan is sowing in their hearts his seed of competitiveness. Jesus has plenty of evidence that all is lost, that with his death his followers will scatter and his teachings be swiftly forgotten. His seed has to all appearances fallen on rocky soil.

He could have chosen to accept that. His mission has failed and God will now destroy this people. Their rejection of the messiah — from his enemies to the apostles—will lead now to a ruin similar to the ruin of Sodom. There are images in Scripture of a God whose patience is at times exhausted.

Jesus can recall the God whom Abraham talks to in the eighteenth chapter of the Book of Genesis. Here is a God set upon the destruction of wicked men. But Abraham intervenes. He suggests, tremulously, that there may be some innocent in Sodom, and God would be then destroying innocent lives with the guilty.

> Do not think of doing such a thing:
> to put the upright to death with the guilty,
> so that upright and guilty fare alike!
> Is the judge of the whole world not to act justly?
> (Gen. 18:25 NJB)

Abraham tries to get God to spare the city, but it is a very nervous Abraham. "I hope the Lord will not be angry if I go on. . . . I trust my Lord will not be angry if I speak once more" (Gen. 18:30,32 NJB).

This is one of the images of God available to Jesus. But it is not the only one. Another book of Scripture, one that we know he enjoyed, has a very different image of God. In it a city is sinful, much like Sodom. Its sins are leading it to sure destruction. But in this case God has no desire to destroy the town. He is determined to save it. He finds a prophet to send in the hope that the city can be saved.

What happens then is a total reversal of the Genesis scene. The prophet does not want this city saved. He wants God to destroy it. In the Genesis account God is set on destruction and a human being tries to get God to be merciful. The God of the Abraham scene needs to be reminded to be compassionate. Abraham is the merciful one.

But in the Book of Jonah the problem is a human being. He wants his fellow human beings punished. It is precisely because God is tender and compassionate, slow to anger and rich in faithful love that Jonah does not want to obey God. He fears that his fellow human beings will get away without punishment. This is not a God who needs to be reminded to be merciful. Just the reverse: it is the man, Jonah, who needs God to keep urging him to forgive.

This image of God is close to Jesus' own. God is not the one who inflicts pain. It is the human being who crucifies his fellow human beings. It is God who uses his full Godhead to deliver us.

Remember again it is by choice that Jesus believes in such a God. The evidence he has that God is like that is the same evidence we have. At this moment in his life, it is rather nonexistent.

There is yet another element in the Jonah story that would have attracted Jesus. Jonah is very honest. He knows what he wants and he tells God so. God gets him so angry because God refuses to do Jonah's will. There is no pretense. He doesn't go to God and say how much he wants to do his will. He is like that son who does not want to work in the field and says so. That kind of honest dealing with God always works out well.

Jesus too knows what he wants. He does not want his mission to collapse. He does not want his career interfered with. He wants his enemies to be foiled. He wants their plans to fail.

God isn't doing the interfering. No. It is people who are getting in Jesus' way. Why should anyone let mere human beings interrupt his mission? Why should that be accepted?

In the prayer in the garden, Jesus speaks of his own will, what he wants done. He knows precisely what he wants, and he knows that it is not what the Father wants. He asks the Father to do what he, Jesus, wants, if it is at all possible.

Of course it is possible. There is a choice. And the choice is within Jesus' freedom. But the consequences of that choice are spelled out. If God intervenes, delivering Jesus in a mighty display, Jesus will be saved. He has imagined the scene. He imagines what will happen if he appeals to the Father:

> Or do you think
> that I cannot appeal to my Father,
> who would promptly send

more than twelve legions of angels
to my defence? (Matt. 26:53 NJB)

He is very conscious that the decision is his. He is also very conscious that the Father does not want Jesus to appeal for such help. He reads the Father's desire in Scripture. He is filled with assurance that the Father wants those texts to be fulfilled in Jesus' dying. He is aware that apart from his dying the people will be lost, all the hopes of the Father to save them will be frustrated.

The experience of Jesus in the garden is called the school of Christian prayer. The first requirement for dialogue with God is honesty. I must be willing to admit that I do have my own desires. I am tempted to say, "All I want is to do your will," when that is far from the case. Jesus is very aware of his own preferences.

Father,
for you everything is possible.
Take this cup away from me. (Mark 14:36 NJB)

Is Jesus aware of what it is like for God to hear him pray like this in agony? Does a strong consciousness come to him of how the Father is feeling as Jesus asks that the cup be taken away? Is the wrenching in the Father's heart revealed to Jesus, how torn the Father is by a desire to hear his Son, the Beloved, and yet to save the people?

What an agony the Father experiences at this moment.

Remember, again, Jesus is coming to this awareness by choosing, by deciding to believe in the reality of just such a Father. He has no more evidence for it than we do.

This openness to believing in a compassionate God frees him to hear the Father's will. The Father wants Jesus to let it all happen and to let them get their way, to trust that the Father will somehow work the salvation of all through this dying. "Let your will be done, not mine" (Luke 22:42 NJB).

Then a strong consolation comes to him. It is not the twelve legions come to intervene. It is a messenger of God. "Then an angel appeared to him, coming from heaven to give him strength" (Luke 22:43 NJB).

The strength that came was to be with him throughout the Passion. The deciding was painful. But now he had decided: The Father is trustworthy.

At some point during his life or at his Resurrection, Jesus becomes aware that he is divine. At some point he feels himself invited to know himself to be the only-begotten Son, the perfect mirror of the Father. Is it during his prayer in the garden that Jesus is led to believe this, that he becomes aware of the full nature of the good news. It is one of the occasions when the evangelist puts on his lips that word *Abba,* a word filled with the trustworthiness of God? God has a secret way of saving people precisely because he has a secret Son, a Son who has been hidden since the foundation of the world.

God invites that Son to become his way of saving the world. Jesus becomes conscious that he is being invited to see himself as that Son. For this reason his death, an ultimate defeat in the terms of the world, will be a fountain of grace and glory. It will be the perfect receptivity to the Father's initiative, the human decision to believe that will mirror fully the Father's trustworthiness. In Jesus' death the Father will be fully revealed to the world as the one who can be trusted even in death.

His death will reveal that God has a gift that triumphs over evil—even over death. That gift is an unshakable trust in God, a childlike, filial faith. It will come to each of us only as a share in the faith decision that Jesus now is making.

Jesus is to see himself in his passion as God become servant, as God become whipping boy. His being scourged is God being scourged. It is the scourging of the divine Son. It is an image so strange and so horrible that it finds no foothold in the human consciousness, even today.

Scripture is filled with the glory of the Day of the Lord. God is to be revealed in immense power. The Elijah figure, a prophet of great power, begins it. Then the messiah himself will come, and his rule will be irresistible.

But other images come to Jesus. An Elijah who is helpless before his enemies and is put to death cheaply. A messiah who is tortured and killed. And now a divine Son whose head is submerged by his enemies until no breath is left in his body! The human consciousness of Jesus puts together God and death. The Alpha and the Omega, the Living One, will die and will be alive forever.

He sees that his human story is a moment in another story. God has his story too, and Jesus' dying will be a moment in God's own life. His decision to let them put him to death, the decision that God is inviting him to make, this decision of his human will, will unleash a divine invasion of the human story. Entry into the divine story, the very being-like-God, will become an option for each of us. An energy source will enter human lives that is the very energy God enjoys.

All this was, we know, to be part of the faith of Christians in the early church. It would be strange if the divine Son himself never realized as much as they did so soon after his death. How such an image and such a story, such an interpretation of his life, succeeded in getting itself believed by anyone is a mystery. But believe it they did. It is not the kind of mind-set that would naturally develop given enough time. It is an incredible view of reality.

But the one human whom we see involved in the coming of this way of believing, and who has any growing disposition for it, is Jesus himself. We see in him an openness to it, a willingness to choose faith in the midst of the most striking lack of evidence. The only scenario for the coming of this revelation offered to us is the experience of Jesus himself.

What is it like to become the host to such thoughts? We are quite aware in our own lives of the mind-boggling effect of faith experiences. To be invited to see ourselves as children of God, dearly loved, can be ours in moments of intense joy. It is a fleeting awareness filled with great warmth. In a sense we never possess it.

Undoubtedly this is the experience of Jesus too. There is a persistent choosing to believe what can be felt only at moments. The angel brings strength, the strength to believe.

Any scenario we project is going to appear unlikely, because the event itself is unlikely to start with. But it did happen. To go ahead without a scenario is to leave Jesus unknown in his concrete individuality, to make of him an angel in human disguise. All we can do is project one of the many possibilities, one of which we know actually happened. It will flesh out our image and enable it to come alive in our imagination.

Once we enter the world of imagining his life, we must make choices; we must imagine him knowing or not knowing. The imagination doesn't allow for keeping the options open. Nor did his actual life.

What was it like for him to enter into the secret hidden from the world since its beginnings, locked away in God's consciousness? In one way such a state is not that hard for humans to imagine. We readily imagine ourselves with superhuman powers; we love films that show that. We fantasize about having superhuman strength or speed or vision or mind-reading ability or knowledge of the future or a more-than-human passing arm or baseball arm or baseball eye.

There is this difference though. This awareness of divine Sonship came to Jesus through his own choice, through his own faith. It was not because he began to experience evidences of immortality within him but because he clearly heard himself promised immortality and was enabled to believe that promise.

A human consciousness becomes more and more flooded with wondrous images. A sense of reality clothes them because of his deliberate openness to the truth. He is caught up more and more in this world so different from the appearances around him. As he is drawn down into a criminal's death at the hands of the hypocrites, he chooses to see himself being invaded by a divine event, an event which through his freedom will become the permanent horizon of human history. An energy is being channeled through him to touch and heal all his brothers and sisters.

Prayer Exercise

Take this one step at a time.

You arrive at the upper room late. The meal has begun. Imagine climbing the staircase, hearing the sounds from above. You enter the room and someone notices and beckons you to sit next to him. All greet you.

After imagining some conversation and eating, read Luke 22:15-20. Close the book and imagine it happening.

Then read Luke 22:24 and imagine how someone makes a remark about some issue that is very important to you, so that you can realistically imagine yourself getting deeply involved in the dispute.

Now continue reading Luke, a verse or two at a time, closing your eyes and imagining it all, with yourself in the middle of it. Next to you Judas leaves, and an apostle you do not like comes to sit.

The meal is coming to an end. You go to the kitchen with two others to start washing the dishes. You can hear a popular hymn that the apostles have begun to sing at the table. The other two leave you alone. You keep on washing. After the song the apostle who annoys you comes to help. A typical friction occurs.

Once it is vividly imagined, let Jesus come into the kitchen and notice and react. Then all go out, by twos and threes, to the garden.

Read Luke 22:39–54, and imagine it all slowly. Always be conscious of the presence of the other disciples.

Put yourself in the presence of God. Use the prayer contained in Eph. 1:3–12.

Let us give thanks to the God and Father of our Lord Jesus Christ! For in our union with Christ God has blessed us by giving us every spiritual blessing in the heavenly world.

Chapter Twenty-Four

What is it like to be nailed to a cross? The evangelists give us some suggestions as they put Psalm 22 in Jesus' mouth. It begins with a powerful mood.

> My God, my God, why have you forsaken me?
> The words of my groaning do nothing to save me,
> My God, I call by day but you do not answer,
> at night, but I find no respite. (Ps. 22:1–2 NJB)

There is going to be a sharp contrast between the things happening around him and his faith that the mood of these events is based on the illusion of appearances. All appears lost, but Jesus chooses otherwise:

> Yet you, the Holy One . . .
> in you our ancestors put their trust,
> they trusted and you set them free.
> To you they called for help and were delivered;
> in you they trusted and were not put to shame.
> (Ps. 22:3–5 NJB)

But he chooses not to call for help. He chooses to let them put him to shame.

> But I am a worm, not a man,
> scorn of mankind, contempt of the people;
> all who see me jeer at me,
> they sneer and wag their heads:
> "He trusted himself to the LORD,
> let the LORD set him free!
> Let him deliver him, as he took such delight in him!"
> (Ps. 22:6–8 NJB)

It so closely fits what is happening around him. It also expresses his conviction that God is decisively triumphing through this dying.

> I shall proclaim your name to my brothers,
> praise you in full assembly:
> "You who fear the LORD, praise him!" (Ps. 22:22 NJB)

This is his praise, this dying. This reveals the secret heart of God, and in being revealed it can touch and heal all.

> The whole wide world will remember
> and return to the LORD,
> all the families of nations bow down before him.
> (Ps. 22:27 NJB)

Jesus goes to his death affirming God's trustworthiness.

> And those who are dead,
> their descendants will serve him,
> will proclaim his name to generations still to come;
> and these will tell of his saving justice
> to a people yet unborn:
> he has fulfilled it. (Ps. 22:30–31 NJB)

What has God fulfilled? To all appearances, nothing. Within Jesus is the assurance that, of course, God is moving forward toward the salvation of all.

It is so much like the stories of the martyrs—lions all about and certain death, but they sing of God's wonderful love and his kind care of them.

What does God do for Jesus? He pours his Spirit into him so fully that Jesus is enabled to believe and to love those who were doing him to death.

What a change is present in Jesus' mood during the Resurrection appearances. It is like the image of him we look forward to meeting as we pass from this world to heaven. The edge is gone from his voice. There is great peace. There is no struggle to choose.

What a joy to him to be able to bring his followers the great news. What a delight to see the effect in them, their incredulity, their joy. Like the beggar who is revealed as king, what joy to reveal to the beggar-friends the majesty that has come close to them. The gospel news can now be seen in its fullness.

We love scenes like this. Some of our great moments of literature involve this revealing of a true and unguessed identity. What a special moment to be the bearer of such spectacular good news to your discouraged friends!

Now he is fully aware of what God was up to—how the human scene is made whole by the coming of someone from another world or, rather, from the foundations of this world. Up from the foundations of our world, that far more intense reality, comes one who reveals to us the basic laws that govern our world, hidden as they are from us.

He had preached—and now he has lived it—that all meaning and glory bubbles up into our lives through our willingness to be forgiving and to let go of our resentments and judgments, through our willingness to identify with our brothers and sisters.

From within, from that more-than-human reality, he has come to us. He has formed a group of followers with a bond strong enough to gather them together after his death. This turns out to be all he had to do.

His life, his mission has succeeded. He knows it now, and they feel his assurance. So Jesus meets them that Easter morning.

It is the Jesus we hope to meet. The Father has sowed this image into our history. It draws us forward.

Even so, there is the human choice. We can refuse to believe. Even among those who saw him—a man come back from the dead—there are those who doubt. How to grow into greater and greater assurance of this approaching blessed encounter with him is the goal of Christian spirituality.

Prayer Exercise

After the burial of Jesus, his followers go to Galilee, their home.

You are waking up in Rebecca's house overlooking the lake. Let your senses come alive. You are still feeling some aches from the long walk from Jerusalem. It was three very sad days. After a while you can hear someone moving about—it must be Martha.

You join her, and over a cup of coffee you both chat in low voices. The last thing you want to do is wake up Sarah.

"Let's go out on the porch." The sky is just beginning to brighten. It is so peaceful. Then you notice the boat as the light hits it. Voices come to you over the water. It's six or seven of the disciples, and they don't sound happy.

Down by the shore are a few scattered people. One man has built a small fire.

Suddenly there is a loud voice behind you. "Isn't it glorious!" She's up. "Isn't it perfect!" She dances about. "Is that the men?" You tell her it is. The morning is spoiled.

Suddenly she says, "That's the Lord!" She points at the man building the fire. Read John 21:4–13 and imagine it slowly.

Enter the presence of God. Use the words of the profession of faith that opens the First Letter of John, the whole of the first chapter.

> Something which is known to have been from the beginning—we have heard it, and seen it with our own eyes, and with our own hands we have touched it. The eternal life which was with the Father—this we have seen.

Epilogue

Is this the way it happened? We cannot know. We have suggestions. The rest is up to our imaginations. One person's imagination can be quite comfortable with what another finds unreal, unimaginable.

"The car is gone. I'll bet Harry came over late last night and moved it."

"I can't believe that. Once he's in bed, he never stirs."

We are constantly trying out scenarios and seeing if we are comfortable with them.

"She will be furious when she finds out."

"I just can't see her getting that upset over a two-dollar phone call."

"You don't know her."

It's very much like the question, What was the color of Jesus' eyes. No color is mentioned. But they were not colorless, like Little Orphan Annie. They were human eyes. And that they were human and could be looked into like any human eyes can make a big difference in getting to know Jesus. His eyes were neither color-less nor did they change for each viewer. They were some specific color, and I may not be particularly attracted by them. It can happen.

They were not otherworldly eyes. We are invited to imagine them. Whether we luckily hit the right color matters little. What counts is that I see human eyes gazing at me.

So too here I have projected a series of images. Did they happen this way? We cannot say. But his life was a series of very concrete events and decisions. That we do know. And there is no grasping who he is unless I grasp his human experience.

As with every human, he will be his past as well as his present. Coming to know him better is getting to see the things he decided not to do as well as those he did. How can we take the total predict-ability out of his life? When we look back, each step seems to follow inevitably from the previous step, each choice looks so obvious. How can we catch some of the flavor of the darkness in which he lived.

That's what we have been trying to do.

His was a fully human journey, wrapped on all sides in darkness. It did not have to go the way it went. It went that way in large part because of the choices he made. So many choices about what to do next, and where, and with whom, and how. That is human life.

None of them mattered as much as his repeated decision to trust the Father, to affirm to the world the Father's undistracted concern and involvement. This choice constitutes the center of his personality. By his faith he becomes the full expression of the divine and opens to us the possibility of becoming God's children.

In accepting his death he becomes perfectly the Son of the most faithful Father.

> Since the children are blood and flesh,
> Jesus likewise had a full share in ours,
>> that by his death
>> he might rob the devil,
>> the prince of death,
>> of his power,
>> and free those
>> who through fear of death
>> had been slaves their whole life long.
> Surely he did not come to help angels,
> but rather the children of Abraham;
> therefore he had to become like his brothers and sisters
> in every way,
> that he might be a merciful and faithful high priest
>> before God
>> on their behalf,
>> to expiate the sins of the people.
> Since he was himself tested through what he suffered,
> he is able to help those who are tempted.
> Therefore, holy brothers and sisters who share a
> heavenly calling,
> fix your eyes on Jesus,
>> the apostle and high priest
>> whom we acknowledge in faith,
>> who was faithful to God who appointed him.
> (Heb. 2:14-3:2 NAB)